The Danielson Group

PO Box 7553 • Princeton, NJ 08543
USA
(609) 921-2366 (phone)
(609) 497-3952 (fax)

 First edition 2011. ISBN: 978-0615597829

THE FRAMEWORK FOR TEACHING
EVALUATION INSTRUMENT

2013 EDITION

CHARLOTTE DANIELSON

TABLE OF CONTENTS

Introduction 3

Domain 1 7

Domain 2 33

Domain 3 57

Domain 4 85

The Framework for Teaching identifies those aspects of a teacher's responsibilities that have been documented through empirical studies and theoretical research as promoting improved student learning. While the Framework is not the only possible description of practice, these responsibilities seek to define what teachers should know and be able to do in the exercise of their profession.

The 1996 Edition

First published by ASCD in 1996, *Enhancing Professional Practice: A Framework for Teaching* was an outgrowth of the research compiled by Educational Testing Service (ETS) for the development of *Praxis III: Classroom Performance Assessments*, an observation-based evaluation of first-year teachers used for the purpose of licensing. The Framework extended this work by examining current research to capture the skills of teaching required not only by novice teachers but by experienced practitioners as well.

The Framework quickly found wide acceptance by teachers, administrators, policymakers, and academics as a comprehensive description of good teaching, including levels of performance—unsatisfactory, basic, proficient, and distinguished—for each of its 22 components.

The 2007 Edition

The 2007 edition of the Framework, also published by ASCD as *Enhancing Professional Practice: A Framework for Teaching*, incorporated several important enhancements. Most importantly, it reflected educational research that had been conducted since 1996; this was fully described in its Appendix, "The Research Foundation." Moreover, the 2007 edition included frameworks for non-classroom specialist positions, such as school librarians, nurses, and counselors. These individuals, while typically part of the teacher bargaining unit in a school district, have very different responsibilities from those of classroom teachers. Therefore, they need their own frameworks, tailored to the details of their work. These frameworks were written to reflect the recommendations of their professional organizations, such as the American Association of School Librarians, but organized according to the same structure as that of the Framework for Teaching: Planning and Preparation, The Environment, Delivery of Service (the equivalent of Instruction), and Professional Responsibilities.

The 2007 edition of the Framework for Teaching retained the architecture of the 1996 edition; in both cases, the complex work of teaching is divided into 4 domains and 22 components. Furthermore, each component is composed of several smaller elements, which serve to further define the component. A few of the components were renamed:

- 1c: "Selecting Instructional Goals" was changed to "Setting Instructional Outcomes."
- 1f: "Assessing Student Learning" was revised to "Designing Student Assessments."
- 3a: "Communicating Clearly and Accurately" was revised to "Communicating with Students."
- 3d: "Providing Feedback to Students" was altered to "Using Assessment in Instruction."
- 4d: "Contributing to the School and District" was changed to "Participating in a Professional Community."

Most of these revisions were simple clarifications to the language. In the case of 4d, for example, the original name implied to some people that "Contributing to the School and District" was an additional responsibility, not integral to the work of teaching; whereas the new name, "Participating in a Professional Community," suggests that it is an essential professional obligation.

However, the revisions to 1f and 3d were significant: the 2007 edition clearly assigned the design of student assessments (1f) to Domain 1: Planning and Preparation, and 3d: Using Assessment in Instruction to Domain 3: Instruction. These distinctions were not as apparent in the 1996 edition.

The 2011 Edition

In 2009, the Bill and Melinda Gates Foundation embarked on the large research project, Measures of Effective Teaching (MET), which entailed the video capture of over 23,000 lessons, analyzed according to five observation protocols, with the results of those analyses (together with other measures) correlated to value-added measures of student learning. The aim of the study was to determine which aspects of a teacher's practice were most highly correlated with high levels of student progress.

The Framework for Teaching was one of the models selected for this large-scale study, which involved the (online) training and certification of hundreds of observers for the purpose of rating the quality of teaching in the lessons. In order to fulfill this obligation, it became necessary to supply additional tools to aid in the training of observers, so that they could make accurate and consistent judgments about teaching practice as demonstrated in the large numbers of videotaped lessons. The following additional tools included:

- *Rubric language tighter even than that of the 2007 edition of the Framework for Teaching.* Furthermore, the levels of performance in the 2011 revision are written at the component, rather than the element, level. While providing less detail, the component-level rubrics capture all the essential information from those at the element level and are far easier to use in evaluation than are those at the element level.
- *"Critical attributes" for each level of performance for each component.* These critical attributes provide essential guidance for observers in distinguishing between practice at adjacent levels of performance. They are of enormous value in training and in the actual work of observation and evaluation.
- *Possible examples for each level of performance for each component.* These examples serve to illustrate the meanings of the rubric language. However, they should be regarded for what they are: possible examples. They are not intended to describe **all** the possible ways in which a certain level of performance might be demonstrated in the classroom; those are, of necessity, particular to each grade and subject. The possible examples simply serve to illustrate what practice might look like in a range of settings.

These enhancements to the Framework for Teaching, while created in response to the demands of the MET study, turned out to be valuable additions to the instrument in all its applications. Practitioners found that the enhancements not only made it easier to determine the level of performance reflected in a classroom for each component of the Framework, but also contributed to judgments that are more accurate and more worthy of confidence. As the stakes in teacher evaluation become higher, this increased accuracy is absolutely essential.

As with the 2007 edition, there were absolutely no changes to the architecture of the 2011 edition. Therefore, those educators who invested resources in learning the language of the 2007 edition simply gained additional tools to help them in the challenging work of applying the Framework to actual classroom teaching.

The 2013 Edition

The principal reason for releasing the 2013 edition of *The Framework for Teaching Evaluation Instrument* was to respond to the instructional implications of the Common Core State Standards (CCSS). Since the CCSS have been adopted in the vast majority of states, it seemed to make sense to explore what these would mean in the classroom.

The CCSS, when fully implemented, will have a profound effect on education in America. They envision, for literacy and mathematics initially, deep engagement by students with important concepts, skills, and perspectives. They emphasize active, rather than passive, learning by students. In all areas, they place a premium on deep conceptual understanding, thinking and reasoning, and the skill of argumentation (students taking a position and supporting it with logic and evidence).

In particular, the CCSS advocate specific recommendations in different curricular areas:

- In ELA and literacy in all fields, a close reading of text and a greater emphasis on nonfiction works in addition to fiction
- In mathematics, a focus on the principal topics in each grade level, with growing fluency and skill in the application of mathematical concepts

To the extent that the CCSS deal with what students should learn in school so they will be prepared for college and careers, the biggest implications are in the areas of curriculum and assessment. Educators and policymakers must revise their curricula and their classroom and district assessments, and must locate instructional materials to support the new learning.

But teachers will also have to acquire new instructional skills in order to bring the CCSS to life for their students. Teaching for deep conceptual understanding, for argumentation, and for logical reasoning have not, after all, been high priorities in most school districts or preparation programs. In most classrooms, students don't take an active role in their own learning, nor do they (respectfully) challenge the thinking of their classmates. All of this will represent a major departure, and therefore a major challenge, for many teachers.

But educators who are familiar with the Framework for Teaching will recognize much in the philosophy of the CCSS that is similar to the underlying concepts of the Framework. After all, the centerpiece of the Framework is student engagement, which is defined not as "busy" or "on task," but as "intellectually active." Learning activities for students may be "hands-on," but they should always be "minds-on." Furthermore, the hallmark of distinguished-level practice in the Framework is that teachers have been able to create a community of learners, in which students assume a large part of the responsibility for the success of a lesson; they make suggestions, initiate improvements, monitor their own learning against clear standards, and serve as resources to one another.

However, despite a deep shared philosophy of teaching and learning between the CCSS and the Framework, there are some specific additions that can be made to the rubric language to bring it into complete alignment; those have been added, particularly in the following domains:

- Domain 1—1c: Setting Instructional Outcomes, 1e: Designing Coherent Instruction, and 1f: Designing Student Assessments
- Domain 3—3a: Communicating with Students, 3b: Using Questioning and Discussion Techniques, 3c: Engaging Students in Learning, and 3d: Using Assessment in Instruction

But because the Framework is a generic instrument, applying to all disciplines, and the CCSS are discipline specific, many of the enhancements to the Framework are located in the possible examples, rather than in the rubric language or critical attributes for each level of performance.

Attentive readers who are deeply familiar with the Framework may notice some slight modifications to the language of the rubrics themselves; this has been done, as in previous revisions, in the interests of clarity. Teaching is highly complex work, and describing it is also challenging; as we receive feedback on confusing words and phrases, we try to improve the wording to minimize ambiguity. But educators who have become familiar with the 2011 version of the Framework, who "speak that language" and may have completed the online training and assessment program produced by Teachscape, should know that none of the revisions would alter the assessments of teaching represented in the videotaped lessons.

DOMAIN 1

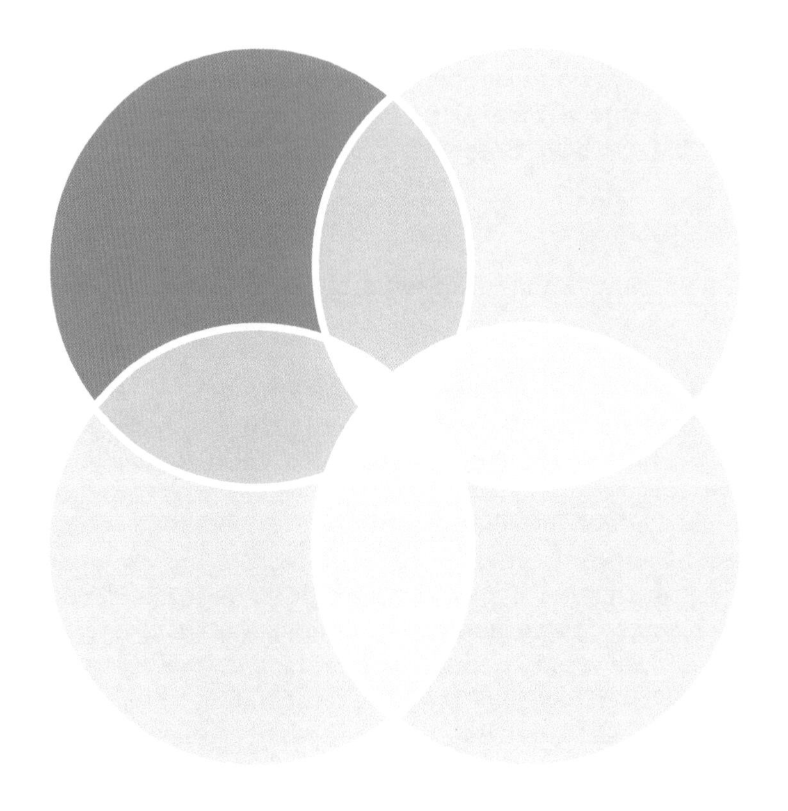

PLANNING AND PREPARATION

1a DEMONSTRATING KNOWLEDGE OF CONTENT AND PEDAGOGY

In order to guide student learning, teachers must have command of the subjects they teach. They must know which concepts and skills are central to a discipline and which are peripheral; they must know how the discipline has evolved into the 21st century, incorporating issues such as global awareness and cultural diversity. Accomplished teachers understand the internal relationships within the disciplines they teach, knowing which concepts and skills are prerequisite to the understanding of others. They are also aware of typical student misconceptions in the discipline and work to dispel them. But knowledge of the content is not sufficient; in advancing student understanding, teachers must be familiar with the particularly pedagogical approaches best suited to each discipline.

The elements of component 1a are:

Knowledge of content and the structure of the discipline

Every discipline has a dominant structure, with smaller components or strands, as well as central concepts and skills.

Knowledge of prerequisite relationships

Some disciplines—for example, mathematics—have important prerequisites; experienced teachers know what these are and how to use them in designing lessons and units.

Knowledge of content-related pedagogy

Different disciplines have "signature pedagogies" that have evolved over time and been found to be most effective in teaching.

Indicators include:

- Lesson and unit plans that reflect important concepts in the discipline
- Lesson and unit plans that accommodate prerequisite relationships among concepts and skills
- Clear and accurate classroom explanations
- Accurate answers to students' questions
- Feedback to students that furthers learning
- Interdisciplinary connections in plans and practice

UNSATISFACTORY • LEVEL 1

In planning and practice, the teacher makes content errors or does not correct errors made by students. The teacher displays little understanding of prerequisite knowledge important to student learning of the content. The teacher displays little or no understanding of the range of pedagogical approaches suitable to student learning of the content.

CRITICAL ATTRIBUTES

- The teacher makes content errors.
- The teacher does not consider prerequisite relationships when planning.
- The teacher's plans use inappropriate strategies for the discipline.

POSSIBLE EXAMPLES

- *The teacher says, "The official language of Brazil is Spanish, just like other South American countries."*
- *The teacher says, "I don't understand why the math book has decimals in the same unit as fractions."*
- *The teacher has his students copy dictionary definitions each week to help them learn to spell difficult words.*
- *And others...*

BASIC • LEVEL 2

The teacher is familiar with the important concepts in the discipline but displays a lack of awareness of how these concepts relate to one another. The teacher indicates some awareness of prerequisite learning, although such knowledge may be inaccurate or incomplete. The teacher's plans and practice reflect a limited range of pedagogical approaches to the discipline or to the students.

CRITICAL ATTRIBUTES

- The teacher's understanding of the discipline is rudimentary.
- The teacher's knowledge of prerequisite relationships is inaccurate or incomplete.
- Lesson and unit plans use limited instructional strategies, and some are not suitable to the content.

POSSIBLE EXAMPLES

- *The teacher plans lessons on area and perimeter independently of one another, without linking the concepts together.*
- *The teacher plans to forge ahead with a lesson on addition with regrouping, even though some students have not fully grasped place value.*
- *The teacher always plans the same routine to study spelling: pretest on Monday, copy the words five times each on Tuesday and Wednesday, test on Friday.*
- *And others...*

PROFICIENT • LEVEL 3

The teacher displays solid knowledge of the important concepts in the discipline and how these relate to one another. The teacher demonstrates accurate understanding of prerequisite relationships among topics. The teacher's plans and practice reflect familiarity with a wide range of effective pedagogical approaches in the subject.

- The teacher can identify important concepts of the discipline and their relationships to one another.
- The teacher provides clear explanations of the content.
- The teacher answers students' questions accurately and provides feedback that furthers their learning.
- Instructional strategies in unit and lesson plans are entirely suitable to the content.

- *The teacher's plan for area and perimeter invites students to determine the shape that will yield the largest area for a given perimeter.*
- *The teacher has realized her students are not sure how to use a compass, and so she plans to have them practice that skill before introducing the activity on angle measurement.*
- *The teacher plans to expand a unit on civics by having students simulate a court trial.*
- *And others...*

DISTINGUISHED • LEVEL 4

The teacher displays extensive knowledge of the important concepts in the discipline and how these relate both to one another and to other disciplines. The teacher demonstrates understanding of prerequisite relationships among topics and concepts and understands the link to necessary cognitive structures that ensure student understanding. The teacher's plans and practice reflect familiarity with a wide range of effective pedagogical approaches in the discipline and the ability to anticipate student misconceptions.

- The teacher cites intra- and interdisciplinary content relationships.
- The teacher's plans demonstrate awareness of possible student misconceptions and how they can be addressed.
- The teacher's plans reflect recent developments in content-related pedagogy.

- *In a unit on 19th-century literature, the teacher incorporates information about the history of the same period.*
- *Before beginning a unit on the solar system, the teacher surveys the students on their beliefs about why it is hotter in the summer than in the winter.*
- *And others...*

DEMONSTRATING KNOWLEDGE OF STUDENTS

Teachers don't teach content in the abstract; they teach it to students. In order to ensure *student* learning, therefore, teachers must know not only their content and its related pedagogy but also the students to whom they wish to teach that content. In ensuring student learning, teachers must appreciate what recent research in cognitive psychology has confirmed, namely, that students learn through active intellectual engagement with content. While there are patterns in cognitive, social, and emotional developmental stages typical of different age groups, students learn in their individual ways and may have gaps or misconceptions that the teacher needs to uncover in order to plan appropriate learning activities. In addition, students have lives beyond school—lives that include athletic and musical pursuits, activities in their neighborhoods, and family and cultural traditions. Students whose first language is not English, as well as students with other special needs, must be considered when a teacher is planning lessons and identifying resources to ensure that all students will be able to learn.

The elements of component 1b are:

Knowledge of child and adolescent development

Children learn differently at different stages of their lives.

Knowledge of the learning process

Learning requires active intellectual engagement.

Knowledge of students' skills, knowledge, and language proficiency

What students are able to learn at any given time is influenced by their level of knowledge and skill.

Knowledge of students' interests and cultural heritage

Children's backgrounds influence their learning.

Knowledge of students' special needs

Children do not all develop in a typical fashion.

Indicators include:

- Formal and informal information about students gathered by the teacher for use in planning instruction
- Student interests and needs learned by the teacher for use in planning
- Teacher participation in community cultural events
- Teacher-designed opportunities for families to share their heritages
- Database of students with special needs

UNSATISFACTORY • LEVEL 1

The teacher displays minimal understanding of how students learn—and little knowledge of their varied approaches to learning, knowledge and skills, special needs, and interests and cultural heritages—and does not indicate that such knowledge is valuable.

CRITICAL ATTRIBUTES

- The teacher does not understand child development characteristics and has unrealistic expectations for students.
- The teacher does not try to ascertain varied ability levels among students in the class.
- The teacher is not aware of students' interests or cultural heritages.
- The teacher takes no responsibility to learn about students' medical or learning disabilities.

POSSIBLE EXAMPLES

- *The lesson plan includes a teacher presentation for an entire 30-minute period to a group of 7-year-olds.*
- *The teacher plans to give her ELL students the same writing assignment she gives the rest of the class.*
- *The teacher plans to teach his class Christmas carols, despite the fact that he has four religions represented among his students.*
- *And others...*

BASIC • LEVEL 2

The teacher displays generally accurate knowledge of how students learn and of their varied approaches to learning, knowledge and skills, special needs, and interests and cultural heritages, yet may apply this knowledge not to individual students but to the class as a whole.

CRITICAL ATTRIBUTES

- The teacher cites developmental theory but does not seek to integrate it into lesson planning.
- The teacher is aware of the different ability levels in the class but tends to teach to the "whole group."
- The teacher recognizes that students have different interests and cultural backgrounds but rarely draws on their contributions or differentiates materials to accommodate those differences.
- The teacher is aware of medical issues and learning disabilities with some students but does not seek to understand the implications of that knowledge.

POSSIBLE EXAMPLES

- *The teacher's lesson plan has the same assignment for the entire class in spite of the fact that one activity is beyond the reach of some students.*
- *In the unit on Mexico, the teacher has not incorporated perspectives from the three Mexican-American children in the class.*
- *Lesson plans make only peripheral reference to students' interests.*
- *The teacher knows that some of her students have IEPs, but they're so long that she hasn't read them yet.*
- *And others...*

PROFICIENT • LEVEL 3

The teacher understands the active nature of student learning and attains information about levels of development for groups of students. The teacher also purposefully acquires knowledge from several sources about groups of students' varied approaches to learning, knowledge and skills, special needs, and interests and cultural heritages.

- The teacher knows, for groups of students, their levels of cognitive development.
- The teacher is aware of the different cultural groups in the class.
- The teacher has a good idea of the range of interests of students in the class.
- The teacher has identified "high," "medium," and "low" groups of students within the class.
- The teacher is well informed about students' cultural heritages and incorporates this knowledge in lesson planning.
- The teacher is aware of the special needs represented by students in the class.

- *The teacher creates an assessment of students' levels of cognitive development.*
- *The teacher examines previous years' cumulative folders to ascertain the proficiency levels of groups of students in the class.*
- *The teacher administers a student interest survey at the beginning of the school year.*
- *The teacher plans activities using his knowledge of students' interests.*
- *The teacher knows that five of her students are in the Garden Club; she plans to have them discuss horticulture as part of the next biology lesson.*
- *The teacher realizes that not all of his students are Christian, and so he plans to read a Hanukkah story in December.*
- *The teacher plans to ask her Spanish-speaking students to discuss their ancestry as part of their social studies unit on South America.*
- *And others...*

DISTINGUISHED • LEVEL 4

The teacher understands the active nature of student learning and acquires information about levels of development for individual students. The teacher also systematically acquires knowledge from several sources about individual students' varied approaches to learning, knowledge and skills, special needs, and interests and cultural heritages.

- The teacher uses ongoing methods to assess students' skill levels and designs instruction accordingly.
- The teacher seeks out information from all students about their cultural heritages.
- The teacher maintains a system of updated student records and incorporates medical and/or learning needs into lesson plans.

- *The teacher plans his lesson with three different follow-up activities, designed to meet the varied ability levels of his students.*
- *The teacher plans to provide multiple project options; each student will select the project that best meets his or her individual approach to learning.*
- *The teacher encourages students to be aware of their individual reading levels and make independent reading choices that will be challenging but not too difficult.*
- *The teacher attends the local Mexican heritage day, meeting several of his students' extended family members.*
- *The teacher regularly creates adapted assessment materials for several students with learning disabilities.*
- *And others...*

SETTING INSTRUCTIONAL OUTCOMES

Teaching is a purposeful activity; even the most imaginative activities are directed toward certain desired learning. Therefore, establishing instructional outcomes entails identifying exactly what students will be expected to learn; the outcomes describe not what students will *do*, but what they will *learn*. The instructional outcomes should reflect important learning and must lend themselves to various forms of assessment through which all students will be able to demonstrate their understanding of the content. Insofar as the outcomes determine the instructional activities, the resources used, their suitability for diverse learners, and the methods of assessment employed, they hold a central place in domain 1.

Learning outcomes may be of a number of different types: factual and procedural knowledge, conceptual understanding, thinking and reasoning skills, and collaborative and communication strategies. In addition, some learning outcomes refer to dispositions; it's important not only that students learn to read but also, educators hope, that they will *like* to read. In addition, experienced teachers are able to link their learning outcomes with outcomes both within their discipline and in other disciplines.

The elements of component 1c are:

Value, sequence, and alignment

Outcomes represent significant learning in the discipline reflecting, where appropriate, the Common Core State Standards.

Clarity

Outcomes must refer to what students will learn, not what they will do, and must permit viable methods of assessment.

Balance

Outcomes should reflect different types of learning, such as knowledge, conceptual understanding, and thinking skills.

Suitability for diverse students

Outcomes must be appropriate for all students in the class.

Indicators include:

- Outcomes of a challenging cognitive level
- Statements of student learning, not student activity
- Outcomes central to the discipline and related to those in other disciplines
- Outcomes permitting assessment of student attainment
- Outcomes differentiated for students of varied ability

UNSATISFACTORY • LEVEL 1

The outcomes represent low expectations for students and lack of rigor, and not all of these outcomes reflect important learning in the discipline. They are stated as student activities, rather than as outcomes for learning. Outcomes reflect only one type of learning and only one discipline or strand and are suitable for only some students.

CRITICAL ATTRIBUTES

- Outcomes lack rigor.
- Outcomes do not represent important learning in the discipline.
- Outcomes are not clear or are stated as activities.
- Outcomes are not suitable for many students in the class.

POSSIBLE EXAMPLES

- *A learning outcome for a fourth-grade class is to make a poster illustrating a poem.*
- *All the outcomes for a ninth-grade history class are based on demonstrating factual knowledge.*
- *The topic of the social studies unit involves the concept of revolutions, but the teacher expects his students to remember only the important dates of battles.*
- *Despite the presence of a number of ELL students in the class, the outcomes state that all writing must be grammatically correct.*
- *None of the science outcomes deals with the students' reading, understanding, or interpretation of the text.*
- *And others...*

BASIC • LEVEL 2

Outcomes represent moderately high expectations and rigor. Some reflect important learning in the discipline and consist of a combination of outcomes and activities. Outcomes reflect several types of learning, but the teacher has made no effort at coordination or integration. Outcomes, based on global assessments of student learning, are suitable for most of the students in the class.

CRITICAL ATTRIBUTES

- Outcomes represent a mixture of low expectations and rigor.
- Some outcomes reflect important learning in the discipline.
- Outcomes are suitable for most of the class.

POSSIBLE EXAMPLES

- *Outcomes consist of understanding the relationship between addition and multiplication and memorizing facts.*
- *The reading outcomes are written with the needs of the "middle" group in mind; however, the advanced students are bored, and some lower-level students are struggling.*
- *Most of the English Language Arts outcomes are based on narrative.*
- *And others...*

PROFICIENT • LEVEL 3

Most outcomes represent rigorous and important learning in the discipline and are clear, are written in the form of student learning, and suggest viable methods of assessment. Outcomes reflect several different types of learning and opportunities for coordination, and they are differentiated, in whatever way is needed, for different groups of students.

- Outcomes represent high expectations and rigor.
- Outcomes are related to "big ideas" of the discipline.
- Outcomes are written in terms of what students will learn rather than do.
- Outcomes represent a range of types: factual knowledge, conceptual understanding, reasoning, social interaction, management, and communication.
- Outcomes, differentiated where necessary, are suitable to groups of students in the class.

- *One of the learning outcomes is for students to "appreciate the aesthetics of 18th-century English poetry."*
- *The outcomes for the history unit include some factual information, as well as a comparison of the perspectives of different groups in the run-up to the Revolutionary War.*
- *The learning outcomes include students defending their interpretation of the story with citations from the text.*
- *And others...*

DISTINGUISHED • LEVEL 4

All outcomes represent high-level learning in the discipline. They are clear, are written in the form of student learning, and permit viable methods of assessment. Outcomes reflect several different types of learning and, where appropriate, represent both coordination and integration. Outcomes are differentiated, in whatever way is needed, for individual students.

- The teacher's plans reference curricular frameworks or blueprints to ensure accurate sequencing.
- The teacher connects outcomes to previous and future learning.
- Outcomes are differentiated to encourage individual students to take educational risks.

- *The teacher encourages his students to set their own goals; he provides them a taxonomy of challenge verbs to help them strive to meet the teacher's higher expectations of them.*
- *Students will develop a concept map that links previous learning goals to those they are currently working on.*
- *Some students identify additional learning.*
- *The teacher reviews the project expectations and modifies some goals to be in line with students' IEP objectives.*
- *One of the outcomes for a social studies unit addresses students analyzing the speech of a political candidate for accuracy and logical consistency.*
- *And others...*

DEMONSTRATING KNOWLEDGE OF RESOURCES

Student learning is enhanced by a teacher's skillful use of resources. Some of these are provided by the school as "official" materials; others are secured by teachers through their own initiative. Resources fall into several different categories: those used in the classroom by students, those available beyond the classroom walls to enhance student learning, resources for teachers to further their own professional knowledge and skill, and resources that can provide noninstructional assistance to students. Teachers recognize the importance of discretion in the selection of resources, selecting those that align directly with the learning outcomes and will be of most use to the students. Accomplished teachers also ensure that the selection of materials and resources is appropriately challenging for every student; texts, for example, are available at various reading levels to make sure all students can gain full access to the content and successfully demonstrate understanding of the learning outcomes. Furthermore, expert teachers look beyond the school for resources to bring their subjects to life and to assist students who need help in both their academic and nonacademic lives.

The elements of component 1d are:

Resources for classroom use

Materials must align with learning outcomes.

Resources to extend content knowledge and pedagogy

Materials that can further teachers' professional knowledge must be available.

Resources for students

Materials must be appropriately challenging.

Indicators include:

- Materials provided by the district
- Materials provided by professional organizations
- A range of texts
- Internet resources
- Community resources
- Ongoing participation by the teacher in professional education courses or professional groups
- Guest speakers

UNSATISFACTORY • LEVEL 1

The teacher is unaware of resources to assist student learning beyond materials provided by the school or district, nor is the teacher aware of resources for expanding one's own professional skill.

CRITICAL ATTRIBUTES

- The teacher uses only district-provided materials, even when more variety would assist some students.
- The teacher does not seek out resources available to expand her own skill.
- Although the teacher is aware of some student needs, he does not inquire about possible resources.

POSSIBLE EXAMPLES

- *For their unit on China, the students find all of their information in the district-supplied textbook.*
- *The teacher is not sure how to teach fractions but doesn't know how he's expected to learn it by himself.*
- *A student says, "It's too bad we can't go to the nature center when we're doing our unit on the environment."*
- *In the literacy classroom, the teacher has provided only narrative works.*
- *And others...*

BASIC • LEVEL 2

The teacher displays some awareness of resources beyond those provided by the school or district for classroom use and for extending one's professional skill but does not seek to expand this knowledge.

CRITICAL ATTRIBUTES

- The teacher uses materials in the school library but does not search beyond the school for resources.
- The teacher participates in content-area workshops offered by the school but does not pursue other professional development.
- The teacher locates materials and resources for students that are available through the school but does not pursue any other avenues.

POSSIBLE EXAMPLES

- *For a unit on ocean life, the teacher really needs more books, but the school library has only three for him to borrow. He does not seek out others from the public library.*
- *The teacher knows she should learn more about literacy development, but the school offered only one professional development day last year.*
- *The teacher thinks his students would benefit from hearing about health safety from a professional; he contacts the school nurse to visit his classroom.*
- *In the second-grade math class, the teacher misuses base 10 blocks in showing students how to represent numbers.*
- *And others...*

PROFICIENT • LEVEL 3

The teacher displays awareness of resources beyond those provided by the school or district, including those on the Internet, for classroom use and for extending one's professional skill, and seeks out such resources.

- Texts are at varied levels.
- Texts are supplemented by guest speakers and field experiences.
- The teacher facilitates the use of Internet resources.
- Resources are multidisciplinary.
- The teacher expands her knowledge through professional learning groups and organizations.
- The teacher pursues options offered by universities.
- The teacher provides lists of resources outside the classroom for students to draw on.

- *The teacher provides her fifth graders a range of nonfiction texts about the American Revolution so that regardless of their reading level, all students can participate in the discussion of important concepts.*
- *The teacher takes an online course on literature to expand her knowledge of great American writers.*
- *The ELA lesson includes a wide range of narrative and informational reading materials.*
- *The teacher distributes a list of summer reading materials that will help prepare his eighth graders' transition to high school.*
- *And others...*

DISTINGUISHED • LEVEL 4

The teacher's knowledge of resources for classroom use and for extending one's professional skill is extensive, including those available through the school or district, in the community, through professional organizations and universities, and on the Internet.

- Texts are matched to student skill level.
- The teacher has ongoing relationships with colleges and universities that support student learning.
- The teacher maintains a log of resources for student reference.
- The teacher pursues apprenticeships to increase discipline knowledge.
- The teacher facilitates student contact with resources outside the classroom.

- *The teacher is not happy with the out-of-date textbook; his students will critique it and write their own material for social studies.*
- *The teacher spends the summer at Dow Chemical learning more about current research so that she can expand her knowledge base for teaching chemistry.*
- *The teacher matches students in her Family and Consumer Science class with local businesses; the students spend time shadowing employees to understand how their classroom skills might be used on the job.*
- *And others...*

DESIGNING COHERENT INSTRUCTION

Designing coherent instruction is the heart of planning, reflecting the teacher's knowledge of content and of the students in the class, the intended outcomes of instruction, and the available resources. Such planning requires that educators have a clear understanding of the state, district, and school expectations for student learning and the skill to translate these into a coherent plan. It also requires that teachers understand the characteristics of the students they teach and the active nature of student learning. Educators must determine how best to sequence instruction in a way that will advance student learning through the required content. Furthermore, such planning requires the thoughtful construction of lessons that contain cognitively engaging learning activities, the incorporation of appropriate resources and materials, and the intentional grouping of students. Proficient practice in this component recognizes that a well-designed instruction plan addresses the learning needs of various groups of students; one size does not fit all. At the distinguished level, the teacher plans instruction that takes into account the specific learning needs of each student and solicits ideas from students on how best to structure the learning. This plan is then implemented in domain 3.

The elements of component 1e are:

Learning activities

Instruction is designed to engage students and advance them through the content.

Instructional materials and resources

Aids to instruction are appropriate to the learning needs of the students.

Instructional groups

Teachers intentionally organize instructional groups to support student learning.

Lesson and unit structure

Teachers produce clear and sequenced lesson and unit structures to advance student learning.

Indicators include:

- Lessons that support instructional outcomes and reflect important concepts
- Instructional maps that indicate relationships to prior learning
- Activities that represent high-level thinking
- Opportunities for student choice
- Use of varied resources
- Thoughtfully planned learning groups
- Structured lesson plans

UNSATISFACTORY • LEVEL 1

Learning activities are poorly aligned with the instructional outcomes, do not follow an organized progression, are not designed to engage students in active intellectual activity, and have unrealistic time allocations. Instructional groups are not suitable to the activities and offer no variety.

CRITICAL ATTRIBUTES

- Learning activities are boring and/or not well aligned to the instructional goals.
- Materials are not engaging or do not meet instructional outcomes.
- Instructional groups do not support learning.
- Lesson plans are not structured or sequenced and are unrealistic in their expectations.

POSSIBLE EXAMPLES

- *After his ninth graders have memorized the parts of the microscope, the teacher plans to have them fill in a worksheet.*
- *The teacher plans to use a 15-year-old textbook as the sole resource for a unit on communism.*
- *The teacher organizes her class in rows, seating the students alphabetically; she plans to have students work all year in groups of four based on where they are sitting.*
- *The teacher's lesson plans are written on sticky notes in his gradebook; they indicate: lecture, activity, or test, along with page numbers in the text.*
- *And others...*

BASIC • LEVEL 2

Some of the learning activities and materials are aligned with the instructional outcomes and represent moderate cognitive challenge, but with no differentiation for different students. Instructional groups partially support the activities, with some variety. The lesson or unit has a recognizable structure; but the progression of activities is uneven, with only some reasonable time allocations.

CRITICAL ATTRIBUTES

- Learning activities are moderately challenging.
- Learning resources are suitable, but there is limited variety.
- Instructional groups are random, or they only partially support objectives.
- Lesson structure is uneven or may be unrealistic about time expectations.

POSSIBLE EXAMPLES

- *After a mini-lesson, the teacher plans to have the whole class play a game to reinforce the skill she taught.*
- *The teacher finds an atlas to use as a supplemental resource during the geography unit.*
- *The teacher always lets students self-select a working group because they behave better when they can choose whom to sit with.*
- *The teacher's lesson plans are well formatted, but the timing for many activities is too short to actually cover the concepts thoroughly.*
- *The plan for the ELA lesson includes only passing attention to students' citing evidence from the text for their interpretation of the short story.*
- *And others...*

PROFICIENT • LEVEL 3

Most of the learning activities are aligned with the instructional outcomes and follow an organized progression suitable to groups of students. The learning activities have reasonable time allocations; they represent significant cognitive challenge, with some differentiation for different groups of students and varied use of instructional groups.

- Learning activities are matched to instructional outcomes.
- Activities provide opportunity for higher-level thinking.
- The teacher provides a variety of appropriately challenging materials and resources.
- Instructional student groups are organized thoughtfully to maximize learning and build on students' strengths.
- The plan for the lesson or unit is well structured, with reasonable time allocations.

- *The teacher reviews her learning activities with a reference to high-level "action verbs" and rewrites some of the activities to increase the challenge level.*
- *The teacher creates a list of historical fiction titles that will expand her students' knowledge of the age of exploration.*
- *The teacher plans for students to complete a project in small groups; he carefully selects group members by their reading level and learning style.*
- *The teacher reviews lesson plans with her principal; they are well structured, with pacing times and activities clearly indicated.*
- *The fourth-grade math unit plan focuses on the key concepts for that level.*
- *And others...*

DISTINGUISHED • LEVEL 4

The sequence of learning activities follows a coherent sequence, is aligned to instructional goals, and is designed to engage students in high-level cognitive activity. These are appropriately differentiated for individual learners. Instructional groups are varied appropriately, with some opportunity for student choice.

- Activities permit student choice.
- Learning experiences connect to other disciplines.
- The teacher provides a variety of appropriately challenging resources that are differentiated for students in the class.
- Lesson plans differentiate for individual student needs.

- *The teacher's unit on ecosystems lists a variety of challenging activities in a menu; the students choose those that suit their approach to learning.*
- *While completing their projects, the students will have access to a wide variety of resources that the teacher has coded by reading level so that students can make the best selections.*
- *After the cooperative group lesson, the students will reflect on their participation and make suggestions.*
- *The lesson plan clearly indicates the concepts taught in the last few lessons; the teacher plans for his students to link the current lesson outcomes to those they previously learned.*
- *The teacher has contributed to a curriculum map that organizes the ELA Common Core State Standards in tenth grade into a coherent curriculum.*
- *And others...*

DESIGNING STUDENT ASSESSMENTS

Good teaching requires both assessment *of* learning and assessment *for* learning. Assessments *of* learning ensure that teachers know that students have learned the intended outcomes. These assessments must be designed in such a manner that they provide evidence of the full range of learning outcomes; that is, the methods needed to assess reasoning skills are different from those for factual knowledge. Furthermore, such assessments may need to be adapted to the particular needs of individual students; an ESL student, for example, may need an alternative method of assessment to allow demonstration of understanding. Assessment *for* learning enables a teacher to incorporate assessments directly into the instructional process and to modify or adapt instruction as needed to ensure student understanding. Such assessments, although used during instruction, must be designed as part of the planning process. These formative assessment strategies are ongoing and may be used by both teachers and students to monitor progress toward understanding the learning outcomes.

The elements of component 1f are:

Congruence with instructional outcomes

Assessments must match learning expectations.

Criteria and standards

Expectations must be clearly defined.

Design of formative assessments

Assessments for learning must be planned as part of the instructional process.

Use for planning

Results of assessment guide future planning.

Indicators include:

- Lesson plans indicating correspondence between assessments and instructional outcomes
- Assessment types suitable to the style of outcome
- Variety of performance opportunities for students
- Modified assessments available for individual students as needed
- Expectations clearly written with descriptors for each level of performance
- Formative assessments designed to inform minute-to-minute decision making by the teacher during instruction

UNSATISFACTORY • LEVEL 1

Assessment procedures are not congruent with instructional outcomes and lack criteria by which student performance will be assessed. The teacher has no plan to incorporate formative assessment in the lesson or unit.

CRITICAL ATTRIBUTES

- Assessments do not match instructional outcomes.
- Assessments lack criteria.
- No formative assessments have been designed.
- Assessment results do not affect future plans.

POSSIBLE EXAMPLES

- *The teacher marks papers on the foundation of the U.S. Constitution mostly on grammar and punctuation; for every mistake, the grade drops from an A to a B, a B to a C, etc.*
- *The teacher says, "What's the difference between formative assessment and the test I give at the end of the unit?"*
- *The teacher says, "The district gave me this entire curriculum to teach, so I just have to keep moving."*
- *And others...*

BASIC • LEVEL 2

Assessment procedures are partially congruent with instructional outcomes. Assessment criteria and standards have been developed, but they are not clear. The teacher's approach to using formative assessment is rudimentary, including only some of the instructional outcomes.

CRITICAL ATTRIBUTES

- Only some of the instructional outcomes are addressed in the planned assessments.
- Assessment criteria are vague.
- Plans refer to the use of formative assessments, but they are not fully developed.
- Assessment results are used to design lesson plans for the whole class, not individual students.

POSSIBLE EXAMPLES

- *The district goal for the unit on Europe is for students to understand geopolitical relationships; the teacher plans to have the students memorize all the country capitals and rivers.*
- *The plan indicates that the teacher will pause to "check for understanding" but does not specify a clear process for accomplishing that goal.*
- *A student asks, "If half the class passed the test, why are we all reviewing the material again?"*
- *And others...*

PROFICIENT • LEVEL 3

All the instructional outcomes may be assessed by the proposed assessment plan; assessment methodologies may have been adapted for groups of students. Assessment criteria and standards are clear. The teacher has a well-developed strategy for using formative assessment and has designed particular approaches to be used.

- All the learning outcomes have a method for assessment.
- Assessment types match learning expectations.
- Plans indicate modified assessments when they are necessary for some students.
- Assessment criteria are clearly written.
- Plans include formative assessments to use during instruction.
- Lesson plans indicate possible adjustments based on formative assessment data.

- *The teacher knows that his students will have to write a persuasive essay on the state assessment; he plans to provide them with experiences developing persuasive writing as preparation.*
- *The teacher has worked on a writing rubric for her research assessment; she has drawn on multiple sources to be sure the levels of expectation will be clearly defined.*
- *The teacher creates a short questionnaire to distribute to his students at the end of class; using their responses, he will organize the students into different groups during the next lesson's activities.*
- *Employing the formative assessment of the previous morning's project, the teacher plans to have five students work on a more challenging one while she works with six other students to reinforce the previous morning's concept.*
- *And others...*

DISTINGUISHED • LEVEL 4

All the instructional outcomes may be assessed by the proposed assessment plan, with clear criteria for assessing student work. The plan contains evidence of student contribution to its development. Assessment methodologies have been adapted for individual students as the need has arisen. The approach to using formative assessment is well designed and includes student as well as teacher use of the assessment information.

- Assessments provide opportunities for student choice.
- Students participate in designing assessments for their own work.
- Teacher-designed assessments are authentic, with real-world application as appropriate.
- Students develop rubrics according to teacher-specified learning objectives.
- Students are actively involved in collecting information from formative assessments and provide input.

- *To teach persuasive writing, the teacher plans to have his class research and write to the principal on an issue that is important to the students: the use of cell phones in class.*
- *The students will write a rubric for their final project on the benefits of solar energy; the teacher has shown them several sample rubrics, and they will refer to those as they create a rubric of their own.*
- *After the lesson the teacher plans to ask students to rate their understanding on a scale of 1 to 5; the students know that their rating will indicate their activity for the next lesson.*
- *The teacher has developed a routine for her class; students know that if they are struggling with a math concept, they sit in a small group with her during workshop time.*
- *And others...*

DOMAIN 2

THE CLASSROOM ENVIRONMENT

2a CREATING AN ENVIRONMENT OF RESPECT AND RAPPORT

An essential skill of teaching is that of managing relationships with students and ensuring that relationships among students are positive and supportive. Teachers create an environment of respect and rapport in their classrooms by the ways they interact with students and by the interactions they encourage and cultivate among students. An important aspect of respect and rapport relates to how the teacher responds to students and how students are permitted to treat one another. Patterns of interactions are critical to the overall tone of the class. In a respectful environment, all students feel valued, safe, and comfortable taking intellectual risks. They do not fear put-downs or ridicule from either the teacher or other students.

"Respect" shown to the teacher by students should be distinguished from students complying with standards of conduct and behavior. Caring interactions among teachers and students are the hallmark of component 2a (Creating an Environment of Respect and Rapport); while adherence to the established classroom rules characterizes success in component 2d (Managing Student Behavior).

The elements of component 2a are:

Teacher interactions with students, including both words and actions

A teacher's interactions with students set the tone for the classroom. Through their interactions, teachers convey that they are interested in and care about their students.

Student interactions with other students, including both words and actions

As important as a teacher's treatment of students is, how students are treated by their classmates is arguably even more important to students. At its worst, poor treatment causes students to feel rejected by their peers. At its best, positive interactions among students are mutually supportive and create an emotionally healthy school environment. Teachers not only model and teach students how to engage in respectful interactions with one another but also acknowledge such interactions.

Indicators include:

- Respectful talk, active listening, and turn-taking
- Acknowledgment of students' backgrounds and lives outside the classroom
- Body language indicative of warmth and caring shown by teacher and students
- Physical proximity
- Politeness and encouragement
- Fairness

UNSATISFACTORY • LEVEL 1

Patterns of classroom interactions, both between teacher and students and among students, are mostly negative, inappropriate, or insensitive to students' ages, cultural backgrounds, and developmental levels. Student interactions are characterized by sarcasm, put-downs, or conflict. The teacher does not deal with disrespectful behavior.

CRITICAL ATTRIBUTES

- The teacher is disrespectful toward students or insensitive to students' ages, cultural backgrounds, and developmental levels.
- Student body language indicates feelings of hurt, discomfort, or insecurity.
- The teacher displays no familiarity with, or caring about, individual students.
- The teacher disregards disrespectful interactions among students.

POSSIBLE EXAMPLES

- *A student slumps in his chair following a comment by the teacher.*
- *Students roll their eyes at a classmate's idea; the teacher does not respond.*
- *Many students talk when the teacher and other students are talking; the teacher does not correct them.*
- *Some students refuse to work with other students.*
- *The teacher does not call students by their names.*
- *And others...*

BASIC • LEVEL 2

Patterns of classroom interactions, both between teacher and students and among students, are generally appropriate but may reflect occasional inconsistencies, favoritism, and disregard for students' ages, cultures, and developmental levels. Students rarely demonstrate disrespect for one another. The teacher attempts to respond to disrespectful behavior, with uneven results. The net result of the interactions is neutral, conveying neither warmth nor conflict.

CRITICAL ATTRIBUTES

- The quality of interactions between teacher and students, or among students, is uneven, with occasional disrespect or insensitivity.
- The teacher attempts to respond to disrespectful behavior among students, with uneven results.
- The teacher attempts to make connections with individual students, but student reactions indicate that these attempts are not entirely successful.

POSSIBLE EXAMPLES

- *Students attend passively to the teacher, but tend to talk, pass notes, etc. when other students are talking.*
- *A few students do not engage with others in the classroom, even when put together in small groups.*
- *Students applaud halfheartedly following a classmate's presentation to the class.*
- *The teacher says, "Don't talk that way to your classmates," but the student shrugs her shoulders.*
- *And others...*

PROFICIENT • LEVEL 3

Teacher-student interactions are friendly and demonstrate general caring and respect. Such interactions are appropriate to the ages, cultures, and developmental levels of the students. Interactions among students are generally polite and respectful, and students exhibit respect for the teacher. The teacher responds successfully to disrespectful behavior among students. The net result of the interactions is polite, respectful, and business-like, though students may be somewhat cautious about taking intellectual risks.

- Talk between teacher and students and among students is uniformly respectful.
- The teacher successfully responds to disrespectful behavior among students.
- Students participate willingly, but may be somewhat hesitant to offer their ideas in front of classmates.
- The teacher makes general connections with individual students.
- Students exhibit respect for the teacher.

- *The teacher greets students by name as they enter the class or during the lesson.*
- *The teacher gets on the same level with students, kneeling, for instance, beside a student working at a desk.*
- *Students attend fully to what the teacher is saying.*
- *Students wait for classmates to finish speaking before beginning to talk.*
- *Students applaud politely following a classmate's presentation to the class.*
- *Students help each other and accept help from each other.*
- *The teacher and students use courtesies such as "please," "thank you," and "excuse me."*
- *The teacher says, "Don't talk that way to your classmates," and the insults stop.*
- *And others...*

DISTINGUISHED • LEVEL 4

Classroom interactions between teacher and students and among students are highly respectful, reflecting genuine warmth, caring, and sensitivity to students as individuals. Students exhibit respect for the teacher and contribute to high levels of civility among all members of the class. The net result is an environment where all students feel valued and are comfortable taking intellectual risks.

- The teacher demonstrates knowledge and caring about individual students' lives beyond the class and school.
- There is no disrespectful behavior among students.
- When necessary, students respectfully correct one another.
- Students participate without fear of put-downs or ridicule from either the teacher or other students.
- The teacher respects and encourages students' efforts.

- *The teacher inquires about a student's soccer game last weekend (or extracurricular activities or hobbies).*
- *Students say "Shhh" to classmates who are talking while the teacher or another student is speaking.*
- *Students clap enthusiastically for one another's presentations for a job well done.*
- *The teacher says, "That's an interesting idea, Josh, but you're forgetting..."*
- *A student questions a classmate, "Didn't you mean _______?" and the classmate reflects and responds, "Oh, maybe you are right!"*
- *And others...*

ESTABLISHING A CULTURE FOR LEARNING

A "culture for learning" refers to the atmosphere in the classroom that reflects the educational importance of the work undertaken by both students and teacher. It describes the norms that govern the interactions among individuals about the activities and assignments, the value of hard work and perseverance, and the general tone of the class. The classroom is characterized by high cognitive energy, by a sense that what is happening there is important, and by a shared belief that it is essential, and rewarding, to get it right. There are high expectations for all students; the classroom is a place where the teacher and students value learning and hard work.

Teachers who are successful in creating a culture for learning know that students are, by their nature, intellectually curious, and that one of the many challenges of teaching is to direct the students' natural energy toward the content of the curriculum. They also know that students derive great satisfaction, and a sense of genuine power, from mastering challenging content in the same way they experience pride in mastering, for example, a difficult physical skill.

Part of a culture of hard work involves precision in thought and language; teachers whose classrooms display such a culture insist that students use language to express their thoughts clearly. An insistence on precision reflects the importance placed, by both teacher and students, on the quality of thinking; this emphasis conveys that the classroom is a business-like place where important work is being undertaken. The classroom atmosphere may be vibrant, even joyful, but it is not frivolous.

The elements of component 2b are:

Importance of the content and of learning

In a classroom with a strong culture for learning, teachers convey the educational value of what the students are learning.

Expectations for learning and achievement

In classrooms with robust cultures for learning, all students receive the message that although the work is challenging, they are capable of achieving it if they are prepared to work hard. A manifestation of teachers' expectations for high student achievement is their insistence on the use of precise language by students.

Student pride in work

When students are convinced of their capabilities, they are willing to devote energy to the task at hand, and they take pride in their accomplishments. This pride is reflected in their interactions with classmates and with the teacher.

Indicators include:

- Belief in the value of what is being learned
- High expectations, supported through both verbal and nonverbal behaviors, for both learning and participation
- Expectation of high-quality work on the part of students
- Expectation and recognition of effort and persistence on the part of students
- High expectations for expression and work products

UNSATISFACTORY • LEVEL 1

The classroom culture is characterized by a lack of teacher or student commitment to learning, and/or little or no investment of student energy in the task at hand. Hard work and the precise use of language are not expected or valued. Medium to low expectations for student achievement are the norm, with high expectations for learning reserved for only one or two students.

CRITICAL ATTRIBUTES

- The teacher conveys that there is little or no purpose for the work, or that the reasons for doing it are due to external factors.
- The teacher conveys to at least some students that the work is too challenging for them.
- Students exhibit little or no pride in their work.
- Students use language incorrectly; the teacher does not correct them.

POSSIBLE EXAMPLES

- *The teacher tells students that they're doing a lesson because it's in the book or is district-mandated.*
- *The teacher says to a student, "Why don't you try this easier problem?"*
- *Students turn in sloppy or incomplete work.*
- *Many students don't engage in an assigned task, and yet the teacher ignores their behavior.*
- *Students have not completed their homework; the teacher does not respond.*
- *And others...*

BASIC • LEVEL 2

The classroom culture is characterized by little commitment to learning by the teacher or students. The teacher appears to be only "going through the motions," and students indicate that they are interested in the completion of a task rather than the quality of the work. The teacher conveys that student success is the result of natural ability rather than hard work, and refers only in passing to the precise use of language. High expectations for learning are reserved for those students thought to have a natural aptitude for the subject.

CRITICAL ATTRIBUTES

- The teacher's energy for the work is neutral, neither indicating a high level of commitment nor ascribing the need to do the work to external forces.
- The teacher conveys high expectations for only some students.
- Students exhibit a limited commitment to complete the work on their own; many students indicate that they are looking for an "easy path."
- The teacher's primary concern appears to be to complete the task at hand.
- The teacher urges, but does not insist, that students use precise language.

POSSIBLE EXAMPLES

- *The teacher says, "Let's get through this."*
- *The teacher says, "I think most of you will be able to do this."*
- *Students consult with one another to determine how to fill in a worksheet, without challenging one another's thinking.*
- *The teacher does not encourage students who are struggling.*
- *Only some students get right to work after an assignment is given or after entering the room.*
- *And others...*

PROFICIENT • LEVEL 3

The classroom culture is a place where learning is valued by all; high expectations for both learning and hard work are the norm for most students. Students understand their role as learners and consistently expend effort to learn. Classroom interactions support learning, hard work, and the precise use of language.

- The teacher communicates the importance of the content and the conviction that with hard work all students can master the material.
- The teacher demonstrates a high regard for students' abilities.
- The teacher conveys an expectation of high levels of student effort.
- Students expend good effort to complete work of high quality.
- The teacher insists on precise use of language by students.

- *The teacher says, "This is important; you'll need to speak grammatical English when you apply for a job."*
- *The teacher says, "This idea is really important! It's central to our understanding of history."*
- *The teacher says, "Let's work on this together; it's hard, but you all will be able to do it well."*
- *The teacher hands a paper back to a student, saying, "I know you can do a better job on this." The student accepts it without complaint.*
- *Students get to work right away when an assignment is given or after entering the room.*
- *And others...*

DISTINGUISHED • LEVEL 4

The classroom culture is a cognitively busy place, characterized by a shared belief in the importance of learning. The teacher conveys high expectations for learning for all students and insists on hard work; students assume responsibility for high quality by initiating improvements, making revisions, adding detail, and/or assisting peers in their precise use of language.

- The teacher communicates passion for the subject.
- The teacher conveys the satisfaction that accompanies a deep understanding of complex content.
- Students indicate through their questions and comments a desire to understand the content.
- Students assist their classmates in understanding the content.
- Students take initiative in improving the quality of their work.
- Students correct one another in their use of language.

- *The teacher says, "It's really fun to find the patterns for factoring polynomials."*
- *A student says, "I don't really understand why it's better to solve this problem that way."*
- *A student asks a classmate to explain a concept or procedure since he didn't quite follow the teacher's explanation.*
- *Students question one another on answers.*
- *A student asks the teacher for permission to redo a piece of work since she now sees how it could be strengthened.*
- *And others...*

MANAGING CLASSROOM PROCEDURES

A smoothly functioning classroom is a prerequisite to good instruction and high levels of student engagement. Teachers establish and monitor routines and procedures for the smooth operation of the classroom and the efficient use of time. Hallmarks of a well-managed classroom are that instructional groups are used effectively, noninstructional tasks are completed efficiently, and transitions between activities and management of materials and supplies are skillfully done in order to maintain momentum and maximize instructional time. The establishment of efficient routines, and teaching students to employ them, may be inferred from the sense that the class "runs itself."

The elements of component 2c are:

Management of instructional groups

Teachers help students to develop the skills to work purposefully and cooperatively in groups or independently, with little supervision from the teacher.

Management of transitions

Many lessons engage students in different types of activities: large group, small group, independent work. It's important that little time is lost as students move from one activity to another; students know the "drill" and execute it seamlessly.

Management of materials and supplies

Experienced teachers have all necessary materials at hand and have taught students to implement routines for distribution and collection of materials with a minimum of disruption to the flow of instruction.

Performance of classroom routines

Overall, little instructional time is lost in activities such as taking attendance, recording the lunch count, or the return of permission slips for a class trip.

Indicators include:

- Smooth functioning of all routines
- Little or no loss of instructional time
- Students playing an important role in carrying out the routines
- Students knowing what to do, where to move

UNSATISFACTORY • LEVEL 1

Much instructional time is lost due to inefficient classroom routines and procedures. There is little or no evidence of the teacher's managing instructional groups and transitions and/or handling of materials and supplies effectively. There is little evidence that students know or follow established routines.

CRITICAL ATTRIBUTES

- Students not working with the teacher are not productively engaged.
- Transitions are disorganized, with much loss of instructional time.
- There do not appear to be any established procedures for distributing and collecting materials.
- A considerable amount of time is spent off task because of unclear procedures.

POSSIBLE EXAMPLES

- *When moving into small groups, students ask questions about where they are supposed to go, whether they should take their chairs, etc.*
- *There are long lines for materials and supplies.*
- *Distributing or collecting supplies is time consuming.*
- *Students bump into one another when lining up or sharpening pencils.*
- *At the beginning of the lesson, roll-taking consumes much time and students are not working on anything.*
- *And others...*

BASIC • LEVEL 2

Some instructional time is lost due to partially effective classroom routines and procedures. The teacher's management of instructional groups and transitions, or handling of materials and supplies, or both, are inconsistent, leading to some disruption of learning. With regular guidance and prompting, students follow established routines.

CRITICAL ATTRIBUTES

- Students not working directly with the teacher are only partially engaged.
- Procedures for transitions seem to have been established, but their operation is not smooth.
- There appear to be established routines for distribution and collection of materials, but students are confused about how to carry them out.
- Classroom routines function unevenly.

POSSIBLE EXAMPLES

- *Some students not working with the teacher are off task.*
- *Transition between large- and small-group activities requires five minutes but is accomplished.*
- *Students ask what they are to do when materials are being distributed or collected.*
- *Students ask clarifying questions about procedures.*
- *Taking attendance is not fully routinized; students are idle while the teacher fills out the attendance form.*
- *And others...*

PROFICIENT • LEVEL 3

There is little loss of instructional time due to effective classroom routines and procedures. The teacher's management of instructional groups and transitions, or handling of materials and supplies, or both, are consistently successful. With minimal guidance and prompting, students follow established classroom routines.

- Students are productively engaged during small-group or independent work.
- Transitions between large- and small-group activities are smooth.
- Routines for distribution and collection of materials and supplies work efficiently.
- Classroom routines function smoothly.

- *In small-group work, students have established roles; they listen to one another, summarizing different views, etc.*
- *Students move directly between large- and small-group activities.*
- *Students get started on an activity while the teacher takes attendance.*
- *The teacher has an established timing device, such as counting down, to signal students to return to their desks.*
- *The teacher has an established attention signal, such as raising a hand or dimming the lights.*
- *One member of each small group collects materials for the table.*
- *There is an established color-coded system indicating where materials should be stored.*
- *Cleanup at the end of a lesson is fast and efficient.*
- *And others...*

DISTINGUISHED • LEVEL 4

Instructional time is maximized due to efficient and seamless classroom routines and procedures. Students take initiative in the management of instructional groups and transitions, and/or the handling of materials and supplies. Routines are well understood and may be initiated by students.

- With minimal prompting by the teacher, students ensure that their time is used productively.
- Students take initiative in distributing and collecting materials efficiently.
- Students themselves ensure that transitions and other routines are accomplished smoothly.

- *Students redirect classmates in small groups not working directly with the teacher to be more efficient in their work.*
- *A student reminds classmates of the roles that they are to play within the group.*
- *A student redirects a classmate to the table he should be at following a transition.*
- *Students propose an improved attention signal.*
- *Students independently check themselves into class on the attendance board.*
- *And others...*

MANAGING STUDENT BEHAVIOR

In order for students to be able to engage deeply with content, the classroom environment must be orderly; the atmosphere must feel business-like and productive, without being authoritarian. In a productive classroom, standards of conduct are clear to students; they know what they are permitted to do and what they can expect of their classmates. Even when their behavior is being corrected, students feel respected; their dignity is not undermined. Skilled teachers regard positive student behavior not as an end in itself, but as a prerequisite to high levels of engagement in content.

The elements of component 2d are:

Expectations

It is clear, either from what the teacher says, or by inference from student actions, that expectations for student conduct have been established and that they are being implemented.

Monitoring of student behavior

Experienced teachers seem to have eyes in the backs of their heads; they are attuned to what's happening in the classroom and can move subtly to help students, when necessary, re-engage with the content being addressed in the lesson. At a high level, such monitoring is preventive and subtle, which may make it challenging to observe.

Response to student misbehavior

Even experienced teachers find that their students occasionally violate one or another of the agreed-upon standards of conduct; how the teacher responds to such infractions is an important mark of the teacher's skill. Accomplished teachers try to understand why students are conducting themselves in such a manner (are they unsure of the content? are they trying to impress their friends?) and respond in a way that respects the dignity of the student. The best responses are those that address misbehavior early in an episode, although doing so is not always possible.

Indicators include:

- Clear standards of conduct, possibly posted, and possibly referred to during a lesson
- Absence of acrimony between teacher and students concerning behavior
- Teacher awareness of student conduct
- Preventive action when needed by the teacher
- Absence of misbehavior
- Reinforcement of positive behavior

	UNSATISFACTORY • LEVEL 1	BASIC • LEVEL 2
	There appear to be no established standards of conduct, or students challenge them. There is little or no teacher monitoring of student behavior, and response to students' misbehavior is repressive or disrespectful of student dignity.	Standards of conduct appear to have been established, but their implementation is inconsistent. The teacher tries, with uneven results, to monitor student behavior and respond to student misbehavior.
CRITICAL ATTRIBUTES	• The classroom environment is chaotic, with no standards of conduct evident. • The teacher does not monitor student behavior. • Some students disrupt the classroom, without apparent teacher awareness or with an ineffective response.	• The teacher attempts to maintain order in the classroom, referring to classroom rules, but with uneven success. • The teacher attempts to keep track of student behavior, but with no apparent system. • The teacher's response to student misbehavior is inconsistent: sometimes harsh, other times lenient.
POSSIBLE EXAMPLES	• *Students are talking among themselves, with no attempt by the teacher to silence them.* • *An object flies through the air, apparently without the teacher's notice.* • *Students are running around the room, resulting in chaos.* • *Students use their phones and other electronic devices; the teacher doesn't attempt to stop them.* • *And others...*	• *Classroom rules are posted, but neither the teacher nor the students refer to them.* • *The teacher repeatedly asks students to take their seats; some ignore her.* • *To one student: "Where's your late pass? Go to the office." To another: "You don't have a late pass? Come in and take your seat; you've missed enough already."* • *And others...*

PROFICIENT • LEVEL 3

Student behavior is generally appropriate. The teacher monitors student behavior against established standards of conduct. Teacher response to student misbehavior is consistent, proportionate, and respectful to students and is effective.

- Standards of conduct appear to have been established and implemented successfully.
- Overall, student behavior is generally appropriate.
- The teacher frequently monitors student behavior.
- The teacher's response to student misbehavior is effective.

- *Upon a nonverbal signal from the teacher, students correct their behavior.*
- *The teacher moves to every section of the classroom, keeping a close eye on student behavior.*
- *The teacher gives a student a "hard look," and the student stops talking to his neighbor.*
- *And others...*

DISTINGUISHED • LEVEL 4

Student behavior is entirely appropriate. Students take an active role in monitoring their own behavior and/or that of other students against standards of conduct. Teacher monitoring of student behavior is subtle and preventive. The teacher's response to student misbehavior is sensitive to individual student needs and respects students' dignity.

- Student behavior is entirely appropriate; any student misbehavior is very minor and swiftly handled.
- The teacher silently and subtly monitors student behavior.
- Students respectfully intervene with classmates at appropriate moments to ensure compliance with standards of conduct.

- *A student suggests a revision to one of the classroom rules.*
- *The teacher notices that some students are talking among themselves and without a word moves nearer to them; the talking stops.*
- *The teacher speaks privately to a student about misbehavior.*
- *A student reminds her classmates of the class rule about chewing gum.*
- *And others...*

2e ORGANIZING PHYSICAL SPACE

The use of the physical environment to promote student learning is a hallmark of an experienced teacher. Its use varies, of course, with the age of the students: in a primary classroom, centers and reading corners may structure class activities; while with older students, the position of chairs and desks can facilitate, or inhibit, rich discussion. Naturally, classrooms must be safe (no dangling wires or dangerous traffic patterns), and all students must be able to see and hear what's going on so that they can participate actively. Both the teacher and students must make effective use of electronics and other technology.

The elements of component 2e are:

Safety and accessibility

Physical safety is a primary consideration of all teachers; no learning can occur if students are unsafe or if they don't have access to the board or other learning resources.

Arrangement of furniture and use of physical resources

Both the physical arrangement of a classroom and the available resources provide opportunities for teachers to advance learning; when these resources are used skillfully, students can engage with the content in a productive manner. At the highest levels of performance, the students themselves contribute to the use or adaptation of the physical environment.

Indicators include:

- Pleasant, inviting atmosphere
- Safe environment
- Accessibility for all students
- Furniture arrangement suitable for the learning activities
- Effective use of physical resources, including computer technology, by both teacher and students

	UNSATISFACTORY • LEVEL 1	BASIC • LEVEL 2
	The classroom environment is unsafe, or learning is not accessible to many. There is poor alignment between the arrangement of furniture and resources, including computer technology, and the lesson activities.	The classroom is safe, and essential learning is accessible to most students. The teacher makes modest use of physical resources, including computer technology. The teacher attempts to adjust the classroom furniture for a lesson or, if necessary, to adjust the lesson to the furniture, but with limited effectiveness.
CRITICAL ATTRIBUTES	• There are physical hazards in the classroom, endangering student safety. • Many students can't see or hear the teacher or see the board. • Available technology is not being used even if it is available and its use would enhance the lesson.	• The physical environment is safe, and most students can see and hear the teacher or see the board. • The physical environment is not an impediment to learning but does not enhance it. • The teacher makes limited use of available technology and other resources.
POSSIBLE EXAMPLES	• *There are electrical cords running around the classroom.* • *There is a pole in the middle of the room; some students can't see the board.* • *A whiteboard is in the classroom, but it is facing the wall.* • *And others...*	• *The teacher ensures that dangerous chemicals are stored safely.* • *The classroom desks remain in two semicircles, requiring students to lean around their classmates during small-group work.* • *The teacher tries to use a computer to illustrate a concept but requires several attempts to make the demonstration work.* • *And others...*

PROFICIENT • LEVEL 3

The classroom is safe, and students have equal access to learning activities; the teacher ensures that the furniture arrangement is appropriate to the learning activities and uses physical resources, including computer technology, effectively.

- The classroom is safe, and all students are able to see and hear the teacher or see the board.
- The classroom is arranged to support the instructional goals and learning activities.
- The teacher makes appropriate use of available technology.

- *There are established guidelines concerning where backpacks are left during class to keep the pathways clear; students comply.*
- *Desks are moved together so that students can work in small groups, or desks are moved into a circle for a class discussion.*
- *The use of an Internet connection extends the lesson.*
- *And others...*

DISTINGUISHED • LEVEL 4

The classroom environment is safe, and learning is accessible to all students, including those with special needs. The teacher makes effective use of physical resources, including computer technology. The teacher ensures that the physical arrangement is appropriate to the learning activities. Students contribute to the use or adaptation of the physical environment to advance learning.

- Modifications are made to the physical environment to accommodate students with special needs.
- There is total alignment between the learning activities and the physical environment.
- Students take the initiative to adjust the physical environment.
- The teacher and students make extensive and imaginative use of available technology.

- *Students ask if they can shift the furniture to better suit small-group work or discussion.*
- *A student closes the door to shut out noise in the corridor or lowers a blind to block the sun from a classmate's eyes.*
- *A student suggests an application of the whiteboard for an activity.*
- *And others...*

DOMAIN 3

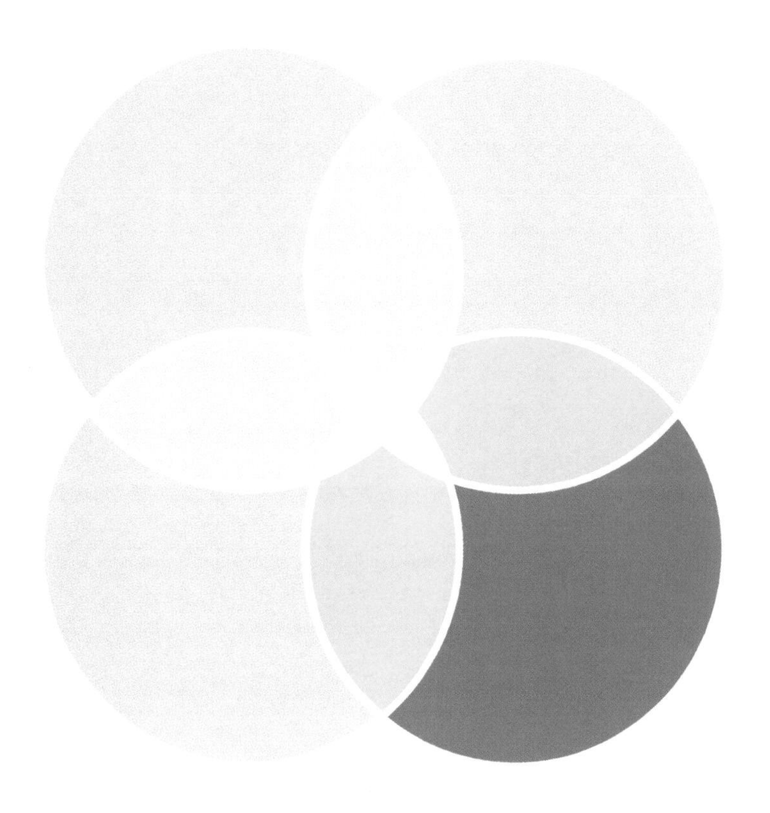

INSTRUCTION

COMMUNICATING WITH STUDENTS

Teachers communicate with students for several independent, but related, purposes. First, they convey that teaching and learning are purposeful activities; they make that purpose clear to students. They also provide clear directions for classroom activities so that students know what to do; when additional help is appropriate, teachers model these activities. When teachers present concepts and information, they make those presentations with accuracy, clarity, and imagination, using precise, academic language; where amplification is important to the lesson, skilled teachers embellish their explanations with analogies or metaphors, linking them to students' interests and prior knowledge. Teachers occasionally withhold information from students (for example, in an inquiry science lesson) to encourage them to think on their own, but what information they do convey is accurate and reflects deep understanding of the content. And teachers' use of language is vivid, rich, and error free, affording the opportunity for students to hear language used well and to extend their own vocabularies. Teachers present complex concepts in ways that provide scaffolding and access to students.

The elements of component 3a are:

Expectations for learning

The goals for learning are communicated clearly to students. Even if the goals are not conveyed at the outset of a lesson (for example, in an inquiry science lesson), by the end of the lesson students are clear about what they have been learning.

Directions for activities

Students understand what they are expected to do during a lesson, particularly if students are working independently or with classmates, without direct teacher supervision. These directions for the lesson's activities may be provided orally, in writing, or in some combination of the two, with modeling by the teacher, if it is appropriate.

Explanations of content

Skilled teachers, when explaining concepts and strategies to students, use vivid language and imaginative analogies and metaphors, connecting explanations to students' interests and lives beyond school. The explanations are clear, with appropriate scaffolding, and, where appropriate, anticipate possible student misconceptions. These teachers invite students to be engaged intellectually and to formulate hypotheses regarding the concepts or strategies being presented.

Use of oral and written language

For many students, their teachers' use of language represents their best model of both accurate syntax and a rich vocabulary; these models enable students to emulate such language, making their own more precise and expressive. Skilled teachers seize on opportunities both to use precise, academic vocabulary and to explain their use of it.

Indicators include:

- Clarity of lesson purpose
- Clear directions and procedures specific to the lesson activities
- Absence of content errors and clear explanations of concepts and strategies
- Correct and imaginative use of language

UNSATISFACTORY • LEVEL 1

The instructional purpose of the lesson is unclear to students, and the directions and procedures are confusing. The teacher's explanation of the content contains major errors and does not include any explanation of strategies students might use. The teacher's spoken or written language contains errors of grammar or syntax. The teacher's academic vocabulary is inappropriate, vague, or used incorrectly, leaving students confused.

CRITICAL ATTRIBUTES

- At no time during the lesson does the teacher convey to students what they will be learning.
- Students indicate through body language or questions that they don't understand the content being presented.
- The teacher makes a serious content error that will affect students' understanding of the lesson.
- Students indicate through their questions that they are confused about the learning task.
- The teacher's communications include errors of vocabulary or usage or imprecise use of academic language.
- The teacher's vocabulary is inappropriate to the age or culture of the students.

POSSIBLE EXAMPLES

- *A student asks, "What are we supposed to be doing?" but the teacher ignores the question.*
- *The teacher states that to add fractions they must have the same numerator.*
- *Students have a quizzical look on their faces; some may withdraw from the lesson.*
- *Students become disruptive or talk among themselves in an effort to follow the lesson.*
- *The teacher uses technical terms without explaining their meanings.*
- *The teacher says "ain't."*
- *And others...*

BASIC • LEVEL 2

The teacher's attempt to explain the instructional purpose has only limited success, and/or directions and procedures must be clarified after initial student confusion. The teacher's explanation of the content may contain minor errors; some portions are clear, others difficult to follow. The teacher's explanation does not invite students to engage intellectually or to understand strategies they might use when working independently. The teacher's spoken language is correct but uses vocabulary that is either limited or not fully appropriate to the students' ages or backgrounds. The teacher rarely takes opportunities to explain academic vocabulary.

CRITICAL ATTRIBUTES

- The teacher provides little elaboration or explanation about what the students will be learning.
- The teacher's explanation of the content consists of a monologue, with minimal participation or intellectual engagement by students.
- The teacher makes no serious content errors but may make minor ones.
- The teacher's explanations of content are purely procedural, with no indication of how students can think strategically.
- The teacher must clarify the learning task so students can complete it.
- The teacher's vocabulary and usage are correct but unimaginative.
- When the teacher attempts to explain academic vocabulary, it is only partially successful.
- The teacher's vocabulary is too advanced, or too juvenile, for students.

POSSIBLE EXAMPLES

- *The teacher mispronounces "______."*
- *The teacher says, "And oh, by the way, today we're going to factor polynomials."*
- *A student asks, "What are we supposed to be doing?" and the teacher clarifies the task.*
- *A student asks, "What do I write here?" in order to complete a task.*
- *The teacher says, "Watch me while I show you how to ______," asking students only to listen.*
- *A number of students do not seem to be following the explanation.*
- *Students are inattentive during the teacher's explanation of content.*
- *Students' use of academic vocabulary is imprecise.*
- *And others...*

PROFICIENT • LEVEL 3

The instructional purpose of the lesson is clearly communicated to students, including where it is situated within broader learning; directions and procedures are explained clearly and may be modeled. The teacher's explanation of content is scaffolded, clear, and accurate and connects with students' knowledge and experience. During the explanation of content, the teacher focuses, as appropriate, on strategies students can use when working independently and invites student intellectual engagement. The teacher's spoken and written language is clear and correct and is suitable to students' ages and interests. The teacher's use of academic vocabulary is precise and serves to extend student understanding.

- The teacher states clearly, at some point during the lesson, what the students will be learning.
- The teacher's explanation of content is clear and invites student participation and thinking.
- The teacher makes no content errors.
- The teacher describes specific strategies students might use, inviting students to interpret them in the context of what they're learning.
- Students engage with the learning task, indicating that they understand what they are to do.
- If appropriate, the teacher models the process to be followed in the task.
- The teacher's vocabulary and usage are correct and entirely suited to the lesson, including, where appropriate, explanations of academic vocabulary.
- The teacher's vocabulary is appropriate to students' ages and levels of development.

- *The teacher says, "By the end of today's lesson you're all going to be able to factor different types of polynomials."*
- *In the course of a presentation of content, the teacher asks students, "Can anyone think of an example of that?"*
- *The teacher uses a board or projection device for task directions so that students can refer to it without requiring the teacher's attention.*
- *The teacher says, "When you're trying to solve a math problem like this, you might think of a similar, but simpler, problem you've done in the past and see whether the same approach would work."*
- *The teacher explains passive solar energy by inviting students to think about the temperature in a closed car on a cold, but sunny, day or about the water in a hose that has been sitting in the sun.*
- *The teacher uses a Venn diagram to illustrate the distinctions between a republic and a democracy.*
- *And others...*

DISTINGUISHED • LEVEL 4

The teacher links the instructional purpose of the lesson to the larger curriculum; the directions and procedures are clear and anticipate possible student misunderstanding. The teacher's explanation of content is thorough and clear, developing conceptual understanding through clear scaffolding and connecting with students' interests. Students contribute to extending the content by explaining concepts to their classmates and suggesting strategies that might be used. The teacher's spoken and written language is expressive, and the teacher finds opportunities to extend students' vocabularies, both within the discipline and for more general use. Students contribute to the correct use of academic vocabulary.

- If asked, students are able to explain what they are learning and where it fits into the larger curriculum context.
- The teacher explains content clearly and imaginatively, using metaphors and analogies to bring content to life.
- The teacher points out possible areas for misunderstanding.
- The teacher invites students to explain the content to their classmates.
- Students suggest other strategies they might use in approaching a challenge or analysis.
- The teacher uses rich language, offering brief vocabulary lessons where appropriate, both for general vocabulary and for the discipline.
- Students use academic language correctly.

- *The teacher says, "Here's a spot where some students have difficulty; be sure to read it carefully."*
- *The teacher asks a student to explain the task to other students.*
- *When clarification about the learning task is needed, a student offers it to classmates.*
- *The teacher, in explaining the westward movement in U.S. history, invites students to consider that historical period from the point of view of the Native Peoples.*
- *The teacher asks, "Who would like to explain this idea to us?"*
- *A student asks, "Is this another way we could think about analogies?"*
- *A student explains an academic term to classmates.*
- *The teacher pauses during an explanation of the civil rights movement to remind students that the prefix* in- *as in* inequality *means "not" and that the prefix* un- *also means the same thing.*
- *A student says to a classmate, "I think that side of the triangle is called the* hypotenuse*."*
- *And others...*

USING QUESTIONING AND DISCUSSION TECHNIQUES

Questioning and discussion are the only instructional strategies specifically referred to in the Framework for Teaching, a decision that reflects their central importance to teachers' practice. In the Framework it is important that questioning and discussion be used as techniques to deepen student understanding rather than serve as recitation, or a verbal "quiz." Good teachers use divergent as well as convergent questions, framed in such a way that they invite students to formulate hypotheses, make connections, or challenge previously held views. Students' responses to questions are valued; effective teachers are especially adept at responding to and building on student responses and making use of their ideas. High-quality questions encourage students to make connections among concepts or events previously believed to be unrelated and to arrive at new understandings of complex material. Effective teachers also pose questions for which they do not know the answers. Even when a question has a limited number of correct responses, the question, being nonformulaic, is likely to promote student thinking.

Class discussions are animated, engaging all students in important issues and promoting the use of precise language to deepen and extend their understanding. These discussions may be based around questions formulated by the students themselves. Furthermore, when a teacher is building on student responses to questions (whether posed by the teacher or by other students), students are challenged to explain their thinking and to cite specific text or other evidence (for example, from a scientific experiment) to back up a position. This focus on argumentation forms the foundation of logical reasoning, a critical skill in all disciplines.

Not all questions must be at a high cognitive level in order for a teacher's performance to be rated at a high level; that is, when exploring a topic, a teacher might begin with a series of questions of low cognitive challenge to provide a review, or to ensure that everyone in the class is "on board." Furthermore, if questions are at a high level, but only a few students participate in the discussion, the teacher's performance on the component cannot be judged to be at a high level. In addition, during lessons involving students in small-group work, the quality of the students' questions and discussion in their small groups may be considered as part of this component. In order for students to formulate high-level questions, they must have learned how to do so. Therefore, high-level questions from students, either in the full class or in small-group discussions, provide evidence that these skills have been taught.

The elements of component 3b are:

Quality of questions/prompts

Questions of high quality cause students to think and reflect, to deepen their understanding, and to test their ideas against those of their classmates. When teachers ask questions of high quality, they ask only a few of them and provide students with sufficient time to think about their responses, to reflect on the comments of their classmates, and to deepen their understanding. Occasionally, for the purposes of review, teachers ask students a series of (usually low-level) questions in a type of verbal quiz. This technique may be helpful for the purpose of establishing the facts of a historical event, for example, but should not be confused with the use of questioning to deepen students' understanding.

Discussion techniques

Effective teachers promote learning through discussion. A foundational skill that students learn through engaging in discussion is that of explaining and justifying their reasoning and conclusions, based on specific evidence. Teachers skilled in the use of questioning and discussion techniques challenge students to examine their premises, to build a logical argument, and to critique the arguments of others. Some teachers report, "We discussed x," when what they mean is "I said x." That is, some teachers confuse discussion with explanation of content; as important as that is, it's not discussion. Rather, in a true discussion a teacher poses a question and invites all students' views to be heard, enabling students to engage in discussion directly with one another, not always mediated by the teacher. Furthermore, in conducting discussions, skilled teachers build further questions on student responses and insist that students examine their premises, build a logical argument, and critique the arguments of others.

Student participation

In some classes a few students tend to dominate the discussion; other students, recognizing this pattern, hold back their contributions. The skilled teacher uses a range of techniques to encourage all students to contribute to the discussion and enlists the assistance of students to ensure this outcome.

Indicators include:

- Questions of high cognitive challenge, formulated by both students and teacher
- Questions with multiple correct answers or multiple approaches, even when there is a single correct response
- Effective use of student responses and ideas
- Discussion, with the teacher stepping out of the central, mediating role
- Focus on the reasoning exhibited by students in discussion, both in give-and-take with the teacher and with their classmates
- High levels of student participation in discussion

UNSATISFACTORY • LEVEL 1

The teacher's questions are of low cognitive challenge, with single correct responses, and are asked in rapid succession. Interaction between the teacher and students is predominantly recitation style, with the teacher mediating all questions and answers; the teacher accepts all contributions without asking students to explain their reasoning. Only a few students participate in the discussion.

CRITICAL ATTRIBUTES

- Questions are rapid-fire and convergent, with a single correct answer.
- Questions do not invite student thinking.
- All discussion is between the teacher and students; students are not invited to speak directly to one another.
- The teacher does not ask students to explain their thinking.
- Only a few students dominate the discussion.

POSSIBLE EXAMPLES

- *All questions are of the "recitation" type, such as "What is 3 x 4?"*
- *The teacher asks a question for which the answer is on the board; students respond by reading it.*
- *The teacher calls only on students who have their hands up.*
- *A student responds to a question with wrong information, and the teacher doesn't follow up.*
- *And others...*

BASIC • LEVEL 2

The teacher's questions lead students through a single path of inquiry, with answers seemingly determined in advance. Alternatively, the teacher attempts to ask some questions designed to engage students in thinking, but only a few students are involved. The teacher attempts to engage all students in the discussion, to encourage them to respond to one another, and to explain their thinking, with uneven results.

CRITICAL ATTRIBUTES

- The teacher frames some questions designed to promote student thinking, but many have a single correct answer, and the teacher calls on students quickly.
- The teacher invites students to respond directly to one another's ideas, but few students respond.
- The teacher calls on many students, but only a small number actually participate in the discussion.
- The teacher asks students to explain their reasoning, but only some students attempt to do so.

POSSIBLE EXAMPLES

- *Many questions are of the "recitation" type, such as "How many members of the House of Representatives are there?"*
- *The teacher asks, "Who has an idea about this?" The usual three students offer comments.*
- *The teacher asks, "Maria, can you comment on Ian's idea?" but Maria does not respond or makes a comment directly to the teacher.*
- *The teacher asks a student to explain his reasoning for why 13 is a prime number but does not follow up when the student falters.*
- *And others...*

PROFICIENT • LEVEL 3

While the teacher may use some low-level questions, he poses questions designed to promote student thinking and understanding. The teacher creates a genuine discussion among students, providing adequate time for students to respond and stepping aside when doing so is appropriate. The teacher challenges students to justify their thinking and successfully engages most students in the discussion, employing a range of strategies to ensure that most students are heard.

- The teacher uses open-ended questions, inviting students to think and/or offer multiple possible answers.
- The teacher makes effective use of wait time.
- Discussions enable students to talk to one another without ongoing mediation by teacher.
- The teacher calls on most students, even those who don't initially volunteer.
- Many students actively engage in the discussion.
- The teacher asks students to justify their reasoning, and most attempt to do so.

- *The teacher asks, "What might have happened if the colonists had not prevailed in the American war for independence?"*
- *The teacher uses the plural form in asking questions, such as "What are some things you think might contribute to _______?"*
- *The teacher asks, "Maria, can you comment on Ian's idea?" and Maria responds directly to Ian.*
- *The teacher poses a question, asking every student to write a brief response and then share it with a partner, before inviting a few to offer their ideas to the entire class.*
- *The teacher asks students when they have formulated an answer to the question "Why do you think Huck Finn did _______?" to find the reason in the text and to explain their thinking to a neighbor.*
- *And others...*

DISTINGUISHED • LEVEL 4

The teacher uses a variety or series of questions or prompts to challenge students cognitively, advance high-level thinking and discourse, and promote metacognition. Students formulate many questions, initiate topics, challenge one another's thinking, and make unsolicited contributions. Students themselves ensure that all voices are heard in the discussion.

- Students initiate higher-order questions.
- The teacher builds on and uses student responses to questions in order to deepen student understanding.
- Students extend the discussion, enriching it.
- Students invite comments from their classmates during a discussion and challenge one another's thinking.
- Virtually all students are engaged in the discussion.

- *A student asks, "How many ways are there to get this answer?"*
- *A student says to a classmate, "I don't think I agree with you on this, because..."*
- *A student asks of other students, "Does anyone have another idea how we might figure this out?"*
- *A student asks, "What if...?"*
- *And others...*

ENGAGING STUDENTS IN LEARNING

Student engagement in learning is the centerpiece of the Framework for Teaching; all other components contribute to it. When students are engaged in learning, they are not merely "busy," nor are they only "on task." Rather, they are intellectually active in learning important and challenging content. The critical distinction between a classroom in which students are compliant and busy, and one in which they are engaged, is that in the latter students are developing their understanding through what they do. That is, they are engaged in discussion, debate, answering "what if?" questions, discovering patterns, and the like. They may be selecting their work from a range of (teacher-arranged) choices, and making important contributions to the intellectual life of the class. Such activities don't typically consume an entire lesson, but they are essential components of engagement.

A lesson in which students are engaged usually has a discernible structure: a beginning, a middle, and an end, with scaffolding provided by the teacher or by the activities themselves. Student tasks are organized to provide cognitive challenge, and then students are encouraged to reflect on what they have done and what they have learned. That is, the lesson has closure, in which teachers encourage students to derive the important learning from the learning tasks, from the discussion, or from what they have read. Critical questions for an observer in determining the degree of student engagement are "What are the students being asked to do? Does the learning task involve thinking? Are students challenged to discern patterns or make predictions?" If the answer to these questions is that students are, for example, filling in blanks on a worksheet or performing a rote procedure, they are unlikely to be cognitively engaged.

In observing a lesson, it is essential not only to watch the teacher but also to pay close attention to the students and what they are doing. The best evidence for student engagement is what students are saying and doing as a consequence of what the teacher does, or has done, or has planned. And while students may be physically active (e.g., using manipulative materials in mathematics or making a map in social studies), it is not essential that they be involved in a hands-on manner; it is, however, essential that they be challenged to be "minds-on."

The elements of component 3c are:

Activities and assignments

The activities and assignments are the centerpiece of student engagement, since they determine what it is that students are asked to do. Activities and assignments that promote learning require student thinking that emphasizes depth over breadth and encourage students to explain their thinking.

Grouping of students

How students are grouped for instruction (whole class, small groups, pairs, individuals) is one of the many decisions teachers make every day. There are many options; students of similar background and skill may be clustered together, or the more-advanced students may be spread around into the different groups. Alternatively, a teacher might permit students to select their own groups, or they could be formed randomly.

Instructional materials and resources

The instructional materials a teacher selects to use in the classroom can have an enormous impact on students' experience. Though some teachers are obliged to use a school's or district's officially sanctioned materials, many teachers use these selectively or supplement them with others of their choosing that are better suited to engaging students in deep learning—for example, the use of primary source materials in social studies.

Structure and pacing

No one, whether an adult or a student, likes to be either bored or rushed in completing a task. Keeping things moving, within a well-defined structure, is one of the marks of an experienced teacher. And since much of student learning results from their reflection on what they have done, a well-designed lesson includes time for reflection and closure.

Indicators include:

- Student enthusiasm, interest, thinking, problem solving, etc.
- Learning tasks that require high-level student thinking and invite students to explain their thinking
- Students highly motivated to work on all tasks and persistent even when the tasks are challenging
- Students actively "working," rather than watching while their teacher "works"
- Suitable pacing of the lesson: neither dragged out nor rushed, with time for closure and student reflection

UNSATISFACTORY • LEVEL 1

The learning tasks/activities, materials, and resources are poorly aligned with the instructional outcomes, or require only rote responses, with only one approach possible. The groupings of students are unsuitable to the activities. The lesson has no clearly defined structure, or the pace of the lesson is too slow or rushed.

CRITICAL ATTRIBUTES

- Few students are intellectually engaged in the lesson.
- Learning tasks/activities and materials require only recall or have a single correct response or method.
- Instructional materials used are unsuitable to the lesson and/or the students.
- The lesson drags or is rushed.
- Only one type of instructional group is used (whole group, small groups) when variety would promote more student engagement.

POSSIBLE EXAMPLES

- *Most students disregard the assignment given by the teacher; it appears to be much too difficult for them.*
- *Students fill out the lesson worksheet by copying words from the board.*
- *Students are using math manipulative materials in a rote activity.*
- *The teacher lectures for 45 minutes.*
- *Most students don't have time to complete the assignment; the teacher moves on in the lesson.*
- *And others...*

BASIC • LEVEL 2

The learning tasks and activities are partially aligned with the instructional outcomes but require only minimal thinking by students and little opportunity for them to explain their thinking, allowing most students to be passive or merely compliant. The groupings of students are moderately suitable to the activities. The lesson has a recognizable structure; however, the pacing of the lesson may not provide students the time needed to be intellectually engaged or may be so slow that many students have a considerable amount of "downtime."

CRITICAL ATTRIBUTES

- Some students are intellectually engaged in the lesson.
- Learning tasks are a mix of those requiring thinking and those requiring recall.
- Student engagement with the content is largely passive; the learning consists primarily of facts or procedures.
- The materials and resources are partially aligned to the lesson objectives.
- Few of the materials and resources require student thinking or ask students to explain their thinking.
- The pacing of the lesson is uneven—suitable in parts but rushed or dragging in others.
- The instructional groupings used are partially appropriate to the activities.

POSSIBLE EXAMPLES

- *Students in only three of the five small groups are figuring out an answer to the assigned problem; the others seem to be unsure how they should proceed.*
- *Students are asked to fill in a worksheet, following an established procedure.*
- *There is a recognizable beginning, middle, and end to the lesson.*
- *The teacher lectures for 20 minutes and provides 15 minutes for the students to write an essay; not all students are able to complete it.*
- *And others...*

PROFICIENT • LEVEL 3

The learning tasks and activities are fully aligned with the instructional outcomes and are designed to challenge student thinking, inviting students to make their thinking visible. This technique results in active intellectual engagement by most students with important and challenging content and with teacher scaffolding to support that engagement. The groupings of students are suitable to the activities. The lesson has a clearly defined structure, and the pacing of the lesson is appropriate, providing most students the time needed to be intellectually engaged.

- Most students are intellectually engaged in the lesson.
- Most learning tasks have multiple correct responses or approaches and/or encourage higher-order thinking.
- Students are invited to explain their thinking as part of completing tasks.
- Materials and resources support the learning goals and require intellectual engagement, as appropriate.
- The pacing of the lesson provides students the time needed to be intellectually engaged.
- The teacher uses groupings that are suitable to the lesson activities.

- *Five students (out of 27) have finished an assignment early and begin talking among themselves; the teacher assigns a follow-up activity.*
- *Students are asked to formulate a hypothesis about what might happen if the American voting system allowed for the direct election of presidents and to explain their reasoning.*
- *Students are given a task to do independently, then to discuss with a table group, followed by a reporting from each table.*
- *Students are asked to create different representations of a large number using a variety of manipulative materials.*
- *The lesson is neither rushed nor does it drag.*
- *And others...*

DISTINGUISHED • LEVEL 4

Virtually all students are intellectually engaged in challenging content through well-designed learning tasks and activities that require complex thinking by students. The teacher provides suitable scaffolding and challenges students to explain their thinking. There is evidence of some student initiation of inquiry and student contributions to the exploration of important content; students may serve as resources for one another. The lesson has a clearly defined structure, and the pacing of the lesson provides students the time needed not only to intellectually engage with and reflect upon their learning but also to consolidate their understanding.

- Virtually all students are intellectually engaged in the lesson.
- Lesson activities require high-level student thinking and explanations of their thinking.
- Students take initiative to improve the lesson by (1) modifying a learning task to make it more meaningful or relevant to their needs, (2) suggesting modifications to the grouping patterns used, and/or (3) suggesting modifications or additions to the materials being used.
- Students have an opportunity for reflection and closure on the lesson to consolidate their understanding.

- *Students are asked to write an essay in the style of Hemmingway and to describe which aspects of his style they have incorporated.*
- *Students determine which of several tools—e.g., a protractor, spreadsheet, or graphing calculator—would be most suitable to solve a math problem.*
- *A student asks whether they might remain in their small groups to complete another section of the activity, rather than work independently.*
- *Students identify or create their own learning materials.*
- *Students summarize their learning from the lesson.*
- *And others...*

USING ASSESSMENT IN INSTRUCTION

Assessment of student learning plays an important new role in teaching: no longer signaling the *end* of instruction, it is now recognized to be an integral *part* of instruction. While assessment *of* learning has always been and will continue to be an important aspect of teaching (it's important for teachers to know whether students have learned what teachers intend), assessment *for* learning has increasingly come to play an important role in classroom practice. And in order to assess student learning for the purposes of instruction, teachers must have a "finger on the pulse" of a lesson, monitoring student understanding and, where feedback is appropriate, offering it to students.

A teacher's actions in monitoring student learning, while they may superficially look the same as those used in monitoring student behavior, have a fundamentally different purpose. When monitoring behavior, teachers are alert to students who may be passing notes or bothering their neighbors; when monitoring student learning, teachers look carefully at what students are writing, or listen carefully to the questions students ask, in order to gauge whether they require additional activity or explanation to grasp the content. In each case, the teacher may be circulating in the room, but his or her purpose in doing so is quite different in the two situations.

Similarly, on the surface, questions asked of students for the purpose of monitoring learning are fundamentally different from those used to build understanding; in the former, the questions seek to reveal students' misconceptions, whereas in the latter the questions are designed to explore relationships or deepen understanding. Indeed, for the purpose of monitoring, many teachers create questions specifically to elicit the extent of student understanding and use additional techniques (such as exit tickets) to determine the degree of understanding of every student in the class. Teachers at high levels of performance in this component, then, demonstrate the ability to encourage students and actually teach them the necessary skills of monitoring their own learning against clear standards.

But as important as monitoring student learning and providing feedback to students are, however, they are greatly strengthened by a teacher's skill in making mid-course corrections when needed, seizing on a "teachable moment," or enlisting students' particular interests to enrich an explanation.

The elements of component 3d are:

Assessment criteria

It is essential that students know the criteria for assessment. At its highest level, students themselves have had a hand in articulating the criteria (for example, of a clear oral presentation).

Monitoring of student learning

A teacher's skill in eliciting evidence of student understanding is one of the true marks of expertise. This is not a hit-or-miss effort, but is planned carefully in advance. Even after planning carefully, however, a teacher must weave monitoring of student learning seamlessly into the lesson, using a variety of techniques.

Feedback to students

Feedback on learning is an essential element of a rich instructional environment; without it, students are constantly guessing at how they are doing and at how their work can be improved. Valuable feedback must be timely, constructive, and substantive and must provide students the guidance they need to improve their performance.

Student self-assessment and monitoring of progress

The culmination of students' assumption of responsibility for their learning is when they monitor their own learning and take appropriate action. Of course, they can do these things only if the criteria for learning are clear and if they have been taught the skills of checking their work against clear criteria.

Indicators include:

- The teacher paying close attention to evidence of student understanding
- The teacher posing specifically created questions to elicit evidence of student understanding
- The teacher circulating to monitor student learning and to offer feedback
- Students assessing their own work against established criteria

UNSATISFACTORY • LEVEL 1

Students do not appear to be aware of the assessment criteria, and there is little or no monitoring of student learning; feedback is absent or of poor quality. Students do not engage in self- or peer assessment.

CRITICAL ATTRIBUTES

- The teacher gives no indication of what high-quality work looks like.
- The teacher makes no effort to determine whether students understand the lesson.
- Students receive no feedback, or feedback is global or directed to only one student.
- The teacher does not ask students to evaluate their own or classmates' work.

POSSIBLE EXAMPLES

- *A student asks, "How is this assignment going to be graded?"*
- *A student asks, "Is this the right way to solve this problem?" but receives no information from the teacher.*
- *The teacher forges ahead with a presentation without checking for understanding.*
- *After the students present their research on globalization, the teacher tells them their letter grade; when students ask how he arrived at the grade, the teacher responds, "After all these years in education, I just know what grade to give."*
- *And others...*

BASIC • LEVEL 2

Students appear to be only partially aware of the assessment criteria, and the teacher monitors student learning for the class as a whole. Questions and assessments are rarely used to diagnose evidence of learning. Feedback to students is general, and few students assess their own work.

CRITICAL ATTRIBUTES

- There is little evidence that the students understand how their work will be evaluated.
- The teacher monitors understanding through a single method, or without eliciting evidence of understanding from students.
- Feedback to students is vague and not oriented toward future improvement of work.
- The teacher makes only minor attempts to engage students in self- or peer assessment.

POSSIBLE EXAMPLES

- *The teacher asks, "Does anyone have a question?*
- *When a student completes a problem on the board, the teacher corrects the student's work without explaining why.*
- *The teacher says, "Good job, everyone."*
- *The teacher, after receiving a correct response from one student, continues without ascertaining whether other students understand the concept.*
- *The students receive their tests back; each one is simply marked with a letter grade at the top.*
- *And others...*

PROFICIENT • LEVEL 3

Students appear to be aware of the assessment criteria, and the teacher monitors student learning for groups of students. Questions and assessments are regularly used to diagnose evidence of learning. Teacher feedback to groups of students is accurate and specific; some students engage in self-assessment.

- The teacher makes the standards of high-quality work clear to students.
- The teacher elicits evidence of student understanding.
- Students are invited to assess their own work and make improvements; most of them do so.
- Feedback includes specific and timely guidance, at least for groups of students.

- *The teacher circulates during small-group or independent work, offering suggestions to students.*
- *The teacher uses specifically formulated questions to elicit evidence of student understanding.*
- *The teacher asks students to look over their papers to correct their errors; most of them engage in this task.*
- *And others...*

DISTINGUISHED • LEVEL 4

Assessment is fully integrated into instruction, through extensive use of formative assessment. Students appear to be aware of, and there is some evidence that they have contributed to, the assessment criteria. Questions and assessments are used regularly to diagnose evidence of learning by individual students. A variety of forms of feedback, from both teacher and peers, is accurate and specific and advances learning. Students self-assess and monitor their own progress. The teacher successfully differentiates instruction to address individual students' misunderstandings.

- Students indicate that they clearly understand the characteristics of high-quality work, and there is evidence that students have helped establish the evaluation criteria.
- The teacher is constantly "taking the pulse" of the class; monitoring of student understanding is sophisticated and continuous and makes use of strategies to elicit information about individual student understanding.
- Students monitor their own understanding, either on their own initiative or as a result of tasks set by the teacher.
- High-quality feedback comes from many sources, including students; it is specific and focused on improvement.

- *The teacher reminds students of the characteristics of high-quality work, observing that the students themselves helped develop them.*
- *While students are working, the teacher circulates, providing specific feedback to individual students.*
- *The teacher uses popsicle sticks or exit tickets to elicit evidence of individual student understanding.*
- *Students offer feedback to their classmates on their work.*
- *Students evaluate a piece of their writing against the writing rubric and confer with the teacher about how it could be improved.*
- *And others...*

DEMONSTRATING FLEXIBILITY AND RESPONSIVENESS

"Flexibility and responsiveness" refer to a teacher's skill in making adjustments in a lesson to respond to changing conditions. When a lesson is well planned, there may be no need for changes during the course of the lesson itself. Shifting the approach in midstream is not always necessary; in fact, with experience comes skill in accurately predicting how a lesson will go and being prepared for different possible scenarios. But even the most skilled, and best prepared, teachers will occasionally find either that a lesson is not proceeding as they would like or that a teachable moment has presented itself. They are ready for such situations. Furthermore, teachers who are committed to the learning of all students persist in their attempts to engage them in learning, even when confronted with initial setbacks.

The elements of component 3e are:

Lesson adjustment

Experienced teachers are able to make both minor and (at times) major adjustments to a lesson, or mid-course corrections. Such adjustments depend on a teacher's store of alternate instructional strategies and the confidence to make a shift when needed.

Response to students

Occasionally during a lesson, an unexpected event will occur that presents a true teachable moment. It is a mark of considerable teacher skill to be able to capitalize on such opportunities.

Persistence

Committed teachers don't give up easily; when students encounter difficulty in learning (which all do at some point), these teachers seek alternate approaches to help their students be successful. In these efforts, teachers display a keen sense of efficacy.

Indicators include:

- Incorporation of students' interests and daily events into a lesson
- The teacher adjusting instruction in response to evidence of student understanding (or lack of it)
- The teacher seizing on a teachable moment

UNSATISFACTORY • LEVEL 1

The teacher ignores students' questions; when students have difficulty learning, the teacher blames them or their home environment for their lack of success. The teacher makes no attempt to adjust the lesson even when students don't understand the content.

CRITICAL ATTRIBUTES

- The teacher ignores indications of student boredom or lack of understanding.
- The teacher brushes aside students' questions.
- The teacher conveys to students that when they have difficulty learning it is their fault.
- In reflecting on practice, the teacher does not indicate that it is important to reach all students.
- The teacher makes no attempt to adjust the lesson in response to student confusion.

POSSIBLE EXAMPLES

- *The teacher says, "We don't have time for that today."*
- *The teacher says, "If you'd just pay attention, you could understand this."*
- *When a student asks the teacher to explain a mathematical procedure again, the teacher says, "Just do the homework assignment; you'll get it then."*
- *And others...*

BASIC • LEVEL 2

The teacher accepts responsibility for the success of all students but has only a limited repertoire of strategies to use. Adjustment of the lesson in response to assessment is minimal or ineffective.

CRITICAL ATTRIBUTES

- The teacher makes perfunctory attempts to incorporate students' questions and interests into the lesson.
- The teacher conveys to students a level of responsibility for their learning but also his uncertainty about how to assist them.
- In reflecting on practice, the teacher indicates the desire to reach all students but does not suggest strategies for doing so.
- The teacher's attempts to adjust the lesson are partially successful.

POSSIBLE EXAMPLES

- *The teacher says, "I'll try to think of another way to come at this and get back to you."*
- *The teacher says, "I realize not everyone understands this, but we can't spend any more time on it."*
- *The teacher rearranges the way the students are grouped in an attempt to help students understand the lesson; the strategy is partially successful.*
- *And others...*

PROFICIENT • LEVEL 3

The teacher successfully accommodates students' questions and interests. Drawing on a broad repertoire of strategies, the teacher persists in seeking approaches for students who have difficulty learning. If impromptu measures are needed, the teacher makes a minor adjustment to the lesson and does so smoothly.

- The teacher incorporates students' interests and questions into the heart of the lesson.
- The teacher conveys to students that she has other approaches to try when the students experience difficulty.
- In reflecting on practice, the teacher cites multiple approaches undertaken to reach students having difficulty.
- When improvising becomes necessary, the teacher makes adjustments to the lesson.

- *The teacher says, "That's an interesting idea; let's see how it fits."*
- *The teacher illustrates a principle of good writing to a student, using his interest in basketball as context.*
- *The teacher says, "This seems to be more difficult for you than I expected; let's try this way," and then uses another approach.*
- *And others...*

DISTINGUISHED • LEVEL 4

The teacher seizes an opportunity to enhance learning, building on a spontaneous event or students' interests, or successfully adjusts and differentiates instruction to address individual student misunderstandings. Using an extensive repertoire of instructional strategies and soliciting additional resources from the school or community, the teacher persists in seeking effective approaches for students who need help.

- The teacher seizes on a teachable moment to enhance a lesson.
- The teacher conveys to students that she won't consider a lesson "finished" until every student understands and that she has a broad range of approaches to use.
- In reflecting on practice, the teacher can cite others in the school and beyond whom he has contacted for assistance in reaching some students.
- The teacher's adjustments to the lesson, when they are needed, are designed to assist individual students.

- *The teacher stops a lesson midstream and says, "This activity doesn't seem to be working. Here's another way I'd like you to try it."*
- *The teacher incorporates the school's upcoming championship game into an explanation of averages.*
- *The teacher says, "If we have to come back to this tomorrow, we will; it's really important that you understand it."*
- *And others...*

DOMAIN 4

PROFESSIONAL RESPONSIBILITIES

REFLECTING ON TEACHING

Reflecting on teaching encompasses the teacher's thinking that follows any instructional event, an analysis of the many decisions made in both the planning and the implementation of a lesson. By considering these elements in light of the impact they had on student learning, teachers can determine where to focus their efforts in making revisions and choose which aspects of the instruction they will continue in future lessons. Teachers may reflect on their practice through collegial conversations, journal writing, examining student work, conversations with students, or simply thinking about their teaching. Reflecting with accuracy and specificity, as well as being able to use in future teaching what has been learned, is an acquired skill; mentors, coaches, and supervisors can help teachers acquire and develop the skill of reflecting on teaching through supportive and deep questioning. Over time, this way of thinking both reflectively and self-critically and of analyzing instruction through the lens of student learning—whether excellent, adequate, or inadequate—becomes a habit of mind, leading to improvement in teaching and learning.

The elements of component 4a are:

Accuracy

As teachers gain experience, their reflections on practice become more accurate, corresponding to the assessments that would be given by an external and unbiased observer. Not only are the reflections accurate, but teachers can provide specific examples from the lesson to support their judgments.

Use in future teaching

If the potential of reflection to improve teaching is to be fully realized, teachers must use their reflections to make adjustments in their practice. As their experience and expertise increases, teachers draw on an ever-increasing repertoire of strategies to inform these adjustments..

Indicators include:

- Accurate reflections on a lesson
- Citation of adjustments to practice that draw on a repertoire of strategies

	UNSATISFACTORY • LEVEL 1	BASIC • LEVEL 2
	The teacher does not know whether a lesson was effective or achieved its instructional outcomes, or the teacher profoundly misjudges the success of a lesson. The teacher has no suggestions for how a lesson could be improved.	The teacher has a generally accurate impression of a lesson's effectiveness and the extent to which instructional outcomes were met. The teacher makes general suggestions about how a lesson could be improved.
CRITICAL ATTRIBUTES	• The teacher considers the lesson but draws incorrect conclusions about its effectiveness. • The teacher makes no suggestions for improvement.	• The teacher has a general sense of whether or not instructional practices were effective. • The teacher offers general modifications for future instruction.
POSSIBLE EXAMPLES	• *Despite evidence to the contrary, the teacher says, "My students did great on that lesson!"* • *The teacher says, "That was awful; I wish I knew what to do!"* • *And others...*	• *At the end of the lesson, the teacher says, "I guess that went okay."* • *The teacher says, "I guess I'll try ______ next time."* • *And others...*

PROFICIENT • LEVEL 3

The teacher makes an accurate assessment of a lesson's effectiveness and the extent to which it achieved its instructional outcomes and can cite general references to support the judgment. The teacher makes a few specific suggestions of what could be tried another time the lesson is taught.

- The teacher accurately assesses the effectiveness of instructional activities used.
- The teacher identifies specific ways in which a lesson might be improved.

- *The teacher says, "I wasn't pleased with the level of engagement of the students."*
- *The teacher's journal indicates several possible lesson improvements.*
- *And others...*

DISTINGUISHED • LEVEL 4

The teacher makes a thoughtful and accurate assessment of a lesson's effectiveness and the extent to which it achieved its instructional outcomes, citing many specific examples from the lesson and weighing the relative strengths of each. Drawing on an extensive repertoire of skills, the teacher offers specific alternative actions, complete with the probable success of different courses of action.

- The teacher's assessment of the lesson is thoughtful and includes specific indicators of effectiveness.
- The teacher's suggestions for improvement draw on an extensive repertoire.

- *The teacher says, "I think that lesson worked pretty well, although I was disappointed in how the group at the back table performed."*
- *In conversation with colleagues, the teacher considers strategies for grouping students differently to improve a lesson.*
- *And others...*

MAINTAINING ACCURATE RECORDS

An essential responsibility of professional educators is keeping accurate records of both instructional and noninstructional events. These include student completion of assignments, student progress in learning, and noninstructional activities that are part of the day-to-day functions in a school setting, such as the return of signed permission slips for a field trip and money for school pictures. Proficiency in this component is vital because these records inform interactions with students and parents and allow teachers to monitor learning and adjust instruction accordingly. The methods of keeping records vary as much as the type of information being recorded. For example, teachers may keep records of formal assessments electronically, using spreadsheets and databases, which allow for item analysis and individualized instruction. A less formal means of keeping track of student progress may include anecdotal notes that are kept in student folders.

The elements of component 4b are:

Student completion of assignments

Most teachers, particularly at the secondary level, need to keep track of student completion of assignments, including not only whether the assignments were actually completed but also students' success in completing them.

Student progress in learning

In order to plan instruction, teachers need to know where each student "is" in his or her learning. This information may be collected formally or informally but must be updated frequently.

Noninstructional records

Noninstructional records encompass all the details of school life for which records must be maintained, particularly if they involve money. Examples include tracking which students have returned their permission slips for a field trip or which students have paid for their school pictures.

Indicators include:

- Routines and systems that track student completion of assignments
- Systems of information regarding student progress against instructional outcomes
- Processes of maintaining accurate noninstructional records

	UNSATISFACTORY • LEVEL 1	BASIC • LEVEL 2
	The teacher's system for maintaining information on student completion of assignments and student progress in learning is nonexistent or in disarray. The teacher's records for noninstructional activities are in disarray, the result being errors and confusion.	The teacher's system for maintaining information on student completion of assignments and student progress in learning is rudimentary and only partially effective. The teacher's records for noninstructional activities are adequate but inefficient and, unless given frequent oversight by the teacher, prone to errors.
CRITICAL ATTRIBUTES	• There is no system for either instructional or noninstructional records. • Record-keeping systems are in disarray and provide incorrect or confusing information.	• The teacher has a process for recording student work completion. However, it may be out of date or may not permit students to access the information. • The teacher's process for tracking student progress is cumbersome to use. • The teacher has a process for tracking some, but not all, noninstructional information, and it may contain some errors.
POSSIBLE EXAMPLES	• *A student says, "I'm sure I turned in that assignment, but the teacher lost it!"* • *The teacher says, "I misplaced the writing samples for my class, but it doesn't matter—I know what the students would have scored."* • *On the morning of the field trip, the teacher discovers that five students never turned in their permission slips.* • *And others...*	• *A student says, "I wasn't in school today, and my teacher's website is out of date, so I don't know what the assignments are!"* • *The teacher says, "I've got all these notes about how the kids are doing; I should put them into the system, but I just don't have time."* • *On the morning of the field trip, the teacher frantically searches all the drawers in the desk looking for the permission slips and finds them just before the bell rings.* • *And others...*

PROFICIENT • LEVEL 3	DISTINGUISHED • LEVEL 4
The teacher's system for maintaining information on student completion of assignments, student progress in learning, and noninstructional records is fully effective.	The teacher's system for maintaining information on student completion of assignments, student progress in learning, and noninstructional records is fully effective. Students contribute information and participate in maintaining the records.
• The teacher's process for recording completion of student work is efficient and effective; students have access to information about completed and/or missing assignments. • The teacher has an efficient and effective process for recording student attainment of learning goals; students are able to see how they're progressing. • The teacher's process for recording noninstructional information is both efficient and effective.	• Students contribute to and maintain records indicating completed and outstanding work assignments. • Students contribute to and maintain data files indicating their own progress in learning. • Students contribute to maintaining noninstructional records for the class.
• *On the class website, the teacher creates a link that students can access to check on any missing assignments.* • *The teacher's gradebook records student progress toward learning goals.* • *The teacher creates a spreadsheet for tracking which students have paid for their school pictures.* • *And others...*	• *A student from each team maintains the database of current and missing assignments for the team.* • *When asked about her progress in a class, a student proudly shows her portfolio of work and can explain how the documents indicate her progress toward learning goals.* • *When they bring in their permission slips for a field trip, students add their own information to the database.* • *And others...*

COMMUNICATING WITH FAMILIES

Although the ability of families to participate in their child's learning varies widely because of other family or job obligations, it is the responsibility of teachers to provide opportunities for them to understand both the instructional program and their child's progress. Teachers establish relationships with families by communicating to them about the instructional program, conferring with them about individual students, and inviting them to be part of the educational process itself. The level of family participation and involvement tends to be greater at the elementary level, when young children are just beginning school. However, the importance of regular communication with families of adolescents cannot be overstated. A teacher's effort to communicate with families conveys the teacher's essential caring, valued by families of students of all ages.

The elements of component 4c are:

Information about the instructional program

The teacher frequently provides information to families about the instructional program.

Information about individual students

The teacher frequently provides information to families about students' individual progress.

Engagement of families in the instructional program

The teacher frequently and successfully offers engagement opportunities to families so that they can participate in the learning activities.

Indicators include:

- Frequent and culturally appropriate information sent home regarding the instructional program and student progress
- Two-way communication between the teacher and families
- Frequent opportunities for families to engage in the learning process

	UNSATISFACTORY • LEVEL 1	BASIC • LEVEL 2
	The teacher provides little information about the instructional program to families; the teacher's communication about students' progress is minimal. The teacher does not respond, or responds insensitively, to parental concerns.	The teacher makes sporadic attempts to communicate with families about the instructional program and about the progress of individual students but does not attempt to engage families in the instructional program. Moreover, the communication that does take place may not be culturally sensitive to those families.
CRITICAL ATTRIBUTES	• Little or no information regarding the instructional program is available to parents. • Families are unaware of their children's progress. • Family engagement activities are lacking. • There is some culturally inappropriate communication.	• School- or district-created materials about the instructional program are sent home. • The teacher sends home infrequent or incomplete information about the instructional program. • The teacher maintains a school-required gradebook but does little else to inform families about student progress. • Some of the teacher's communications are inappropriate to families' cultural norms.
POSSIBLE EXAMPLES	• *A parent says, "I'd like to know what my kid is working on at school."* • *A parent says, "I wish I could know something about my child's progress before the report card comes out."* • *A parent says, "I wonder why we never see any schoolwork come home."* • *And others...*	• *A parent says, "I received the district pamphlet on the reading program, but I wonder how it's being taught in my child's class."* • *A parent says, "I emailed the teacher about my child's struggles with math, but all I got back was a note saying that he's doing fine."* • *The teacher sends home weekly quizzes for parent or guardian signature.* • *And others...*

PROFICIENT • LEVEL 3

The teacher provides frequent and appropriate information to families about the instructional program and conveys information about individual student progress in a culturally sensitive manner. The teacher makes some attempts to engage families in the instructional program.

- The teacher regularly makes information about the instructional program available.
- The teacher regularly sends home information about student progress.
- The teacher develops activities designed to engage families successfully and appropriately in their children's learning.
- Most of the teacher's communications are appropriate to families' cultural norms.

- *The teacher sends a weekly newsletter home to families that describe current class activities, community and/or school projects, field trips, etc.*
- *The teacher creates a monthly progress report, which is sent home for each student.*
- *The teacher sends home a project that asks students to interview a family member about growing up during the 1950s.*
- *And others...*

DISTINGUISHED • LEVEL 4

The teacher communicates frequently with families in a culturally sensitive manner, with students contributing to the communication. The teacher responds to family concerns with professional and cultural sensitivity. The teacher's efforts to engage families in the instructional program are frequent and successful.

- Students regularly develop materials to inform their families about the instructional program.
- Students maintain accurate records about their individual learning progress and frequently share this information with families.
- Students contribute to regular and ongoing projects designed to engage families in the learning process.
- All of the teacher's communications are highly sensitive to families' cultural norms.

- *Students create materials for Back-to-School Night that outline the approach for learning science.*
- *Each student's daily reflection log describes what she or he is learning, and the log goes home each week for review by a parent or guardian.*
- *Students design a project on charting their family's use of plastics.*
- *And others...*

PARTICIPATING IN THE PROFESSIONAL COMMUNITY

Schools are, first of all, environments to promote the learning of students. But in promoting student learning, teachers must work with their colleagues to share strategies, plan joint efforts, and plan for the success of individual students. Schools are, in other words, professional organizations for teachers, with their full potential realized only when teachers regard themselves as members of a professional community. This community is characterized by mutual support and respect, as well as by recognition of the responsibility of all teachers to be constantly seeking ways to improve their practice and to contribute to the life of the school. Inevitably, teachers' duties extend beyond the doors of their classrooms and include activities related to the entire school or larger district, or both. These activities include such things as school and district curriculum committees or engagement with the parent-teacher organization. With experience, teachers assume leadership roles in these activities.

The elements of component 4d are:

Relationships with colleagues

Teachers maintain professional collegial relationships that encourage sharing, planning, and working together toward improved instructional skill and student success.

Involvement in a culture of professional inquiry

Teachers contribute to and participate in a learning community that supports and respects its members' efforts to improve practice.

Service to the school

Teachers' efforts move beyond classroom duties by contributing to school initiatives and projects.

Participation in school and district projects

Teachers contribute to and support larger school and district projects designed to improve the professional community.

Indicators include:

- Regular teacher participation with colleagues to share and plan for student success
- Regular teacher participation in professional courses or communities that emphasize improving practice
- Regular teacher participation in school initiatives
- Regular teacher participation in and support of community initiatives

UNSATISFACTORY • LEVEL 1

The teacher's relationships with colleagues are negative or self-serving. The teacher avoids participation in a professional culture of inquiry, resisting opportunities to become involved. The teacher avoids becoming involved in school events or school and district projects.

CRITICAL ATTRIBUTES

- The teacher's relationships with colleagues are characterized by negativity or combativeness.
- The teacher purposefully avoids contributing to activities promoting professional inquiry.
- The teacher avoids involvement in school activities and district and community projects.

POSSIBLE EXAMPLES

- *The teacher doesn't share test-taking strategies with his colleagues. He figures that if his students do well, he will look good.*
- *The teacher does not attend PLC meetings.*
- *The teacher does not attend any school functions after the dismissal bell.*
- *The teacher says, "I work from 8:30 to 3:30 and not a minute more. I won't serve on any district committee unless they get me a substitute to cover my class."*
- *And others...*

BASIC • LEVEL 2

The teacher maintains cordial relationships with colleagues to fulfill duties that the school or district requires. The teacher participates in the school's culture of professional inquiry when invited to do so. The teacher participates in school events and school and district projects when specifically asked.

CRITICAL ATTRIBUTES

- The teacher has cordial relationships with colleagues.
- When invited, the teacher participates in activities related to professional inquiry.
- When asked, the teacher participates in school activities, as well as district and community projects.

POSSIBLE EXAMPLES

- *The teacher is polite but seldom shares any instructional materials with his grade partners.*
- *The teacher attends PLC meetings only when reminded by her supervisor.*
- *The principal says, "I wish I didn't have to ask the teacher to 'volunteer' every time we need someone to chaperone the dance."*
- *The teacher contributes to the district literacy committee only when requested to do so by the principal.*
- *And others...*

PROFICIENT • LEVEL 3	DISTINGUISHED • LEVEL 4
The teacher's relationships with colleagues are characterized by mutual support and cooperation; the teacher actively participates in a culture of professional inquiry. The teacher volunteers to participate in school events and in school and district projects, making a substantial contribution.	The teacher's relationships with colleagues are characterized by mutual support and cooperation, with the teacher taking initiative in assuming leadership among the faculty. The teacher takes a leadership role in promoting a culture of professional inquiry. The teacher volunteers to participate in school events and district projects, making a substantial contribution and assuming a leadership role in at least one aspect of school or district life.
• The teacher has supportive and collaborative relationships with colleagues. • The teacher regularly participates in activities related to professional inquiry. • The teacher frequently volunteers to participate in school events and school district and community projects.	• The teacher takes a leadership role in promoting activities related to professional inquiry. • The teacher regularly contributes to and leads events that positively impact school life. • The teacher regularly contributes to and leads significant district and community projects.
• *The principal remarks that the teacher's students have been noticeably successful since her teacher team has been focusing on instructional strategies during its meetings.* • *The teacher has decided to take some free MIT courses online and to share his learning with colleagues.* • *The basketball coach is usually willing to chaperone the ninth-grade dance because she knows all of her players will be there.* • *The teacher enthusiastically represents the school during the district social studies review and brings his substantial knowledge of U.S. history to the course writing team.* • *And others...*	• *The teacher leads the group of mentor teachers at school, which is devoted to supporting teachers during their first years of teaching.* • *The teacher hosts a book study group that meets monthly; he guides the book choices so that the group can focus on topics that will enhance their skills.* • *The teacher leads the annual "Olympics" day, thereby involving the entire student body and faculty in athletic events.* • *The teacher leads the district wellness committee, and involves healthcare and nutrition specialists from the community.* • *And others...*

GROWING AND DEVELOPING PROFESSIONALLY

As in other professions, the complexity of teaching requires continued growth and development in order for teachers to remain current. Continuing to stay informed and increasing their skills allows teachers to become ever more effective and to exercise leadership among their colleagues. The academic disciplines themselves evolve, and educators constantly refine their understanding of how to engage students in learning; thus, growth in content, pedagogy, and information technology are essential to good teaching. Networking with colleagues through such activities as joint planning, study groups, and lesson study provides opportunities for teachers to learn from one another. These activities allow for job-embedded professional development. In addition, professional educators increase their effectiveness in the classroom by belonging to professional organizations, reading professional journals, attending educational conferences, and taking university classes. As they gain experience and expertise, educators find ways to contribute to their colleagues and to the profession.

The elements of component 4e are:

Enhancement of content knowledge and pedagogical skill

Teachers remain current by taking courses, reading professional literature, and remaining current on the evolution of thinking regarding instruction.

Receptivity to feedback from colleagues

Teachers actively pursue networks that provide collegial support and feedback.

Service to the profession

Teachers are active in professional organizations in order to enhance both their personal practice and their ability to provide leadership and support to colleagues.

Indicators include:

- Frequent teacher attendance in courses and workshops; regular academic reading
- Participation in learning networks with colleagues; freely shared insights
- Participation in professional organizations supporting academic inquiry

UNSATISFACTORY • LEVEL 1

The teacher engages in no professional development activities to enhance knowledge or skill. The teacher resists feedback on teaching performance from either supervisors or more experienced colleagues. The teacher makes no effort to share knowledge with others or to assume professional responsibilities.

CRITICAL ATTRIBUTES

- The teacher is not involved in any activity that might enhance knowledge or skill.
- The teacher purposefully resists discussing performance with supervisors or colleagues.
- The teacher ignores invitations to join professional organizations or attend conferences.

POSSIBLE EXAMPLES

- *The teacher never takes continuing education courses, even though the credits would increase his salary.*
- *The teacher endures the principal's annual observations in her classroom, knowing that if she waits long enough, the principal will eventually leave and she will be able to simply discard the feedback form.*
- *Despite teaching high school honors mathematics, the teacher declines to join NCTM because it costs too much and makes too many demands on members' time.*
- *And others...*

BASIC • LEVEL 2

The teacher participates to a limited extent in professional activities when they are convenient. The teacher engages in a limited way with colleagues and supervisors in professional conversation about practice, including some feedback on teaching performance. The teacher finds limited ways to assist other teachers and contribute to the profession.

CRITICAL ATTRIBUTES

- The teacher participates in professional activities when they are required or provided by the district.
- The teacher reluctantly accepts feedback from supervisors and colleagues.
- The teacher contributes in a limited fashion to professional organizations.

POSSIBLE EXAMPLES

- *The teacher politely attends district workshops and professional development days but doesn't make much use of the materials received.*
- *The teacher listens to his principal's feedback after a lesson but isn't sure that the recommendations really apply in his situation.*
- *The teacher joins the local chapter of the American Library Association because she might benefit from the free books—but otherwise doesn't feel it's worth much of her time.*
- *And others...*

PROFICIENT • LEVEL 3

The teacher seeks out opportunities for professional development to enhance content knowledge and pedagogical skill. The teacher actively engages with colleagues and supervisors in professional conversation about practice, including feedback about practice. The teacher participates actively in assisting other educators and looks for ways to contribute to the profession.

- The teacher seeks regular opportunities for continued professional development.
- The teacher welcomes colleagues and supervisors into the classroom for the purposes of gaining insight from their feedback.
- The teacher actively participates in organizations designed to contribute to the profession.

- *The teacher eagerly attends the district's optional summer workshops, knowing they provide a wealth of instructional strategies he'll be able to use during the school year.*
- *The teacher enjoys her principal's weekly walk-through visits because they always lead to a valuable informal discussion during lunch the next day.*
- *The teacher joins a science education partnership and finds that it provides him access to resources for his classroom that truly benefit his students.*
- *And others...*

DISTINGUISHED • LEVEL 4

The teacher seeks out opportunities for professional development and makes a systematic effort to conduct action research. The teacher solicits feedback on practice from both supervisors and colleagues. The teacher initiates important activities to contribute to the profession.

- The teacher seeks regular opportunities for continued professional development, including initiating action research.
- The teacher actively seeks feedback from supervisors and colleagues.
- The teacher takes an active leadership role in professional organizations in order to contribute to the profession.

- *The teacher's principal rarely spends time observing in her classroom. Therefore, she has initiated an action research project in order to improve her own instruction.*
- *The teacher is working on a particular instructional strategy and asks his colleagues to observe in his classroom in order to provide objective feedback on his progress.*
- *The teacher has founded a local organization devoted to literacy education; her leadership has inspired teachers in the community to work on several curriculum and instruction projects.*
- *And others...*

SHOWING PROFESSIONALISM

Expert teachers demonstrate professionalism in service both to students and to the profession. Teaching at the highest levels of performance in this component is student focused, putting students first regardless of how this stance might challenge long-held assumptions, past practice, or simply the easier or more convenient procedure. Accomplished teachers have a strong moral compass and are guided by what is in the best interest of each student. They display professionalism in a number of ways. For example, they conduct interactions with colleagues in a manner notable for honesty and integrity. Furthermore, they know their students' needs and can readily access resources with which to step in and provide help that may extend beyond the classroom. Seeking greater flexibility in the ways school rules and policies are applied, expert teachers advocate for their students in ways that might challenge traditional views and the educational establishment. They also display professionalism in the ways they approach problem solving and decision making, with student needs constantly in mind. Finally, accomplished teachers consistently adhere to school and district policies and procedures but are willing to work to improve those that may be outdated or ineffective.

The elements of component 4f are:

Integrity and ethical conduct

Teachers act with integrity and honesty.

Service to students

Teachers put students first in all considerations of their practice.

Advocacy

Teachers support their students' best interests, even in the face of traditional practice or beliefs.

Decision making

Teachers solve problems with students' needs as a priority.

Compliance with school and district regulations

Teachers adhere to policies and established procedures.

Indicators include:

- The teacher having a reputation as being trustworthy and often sought as a sounding board
- The teacher frequently reminding participants during committee or planning work that students are the highest priority
- The teacher supporting students, even in the face of difficult situations or conflicting policies
- The teacher challenging existing practice in order to put students first
- The teacher consistently fulfilling district mandates regarding policies and procedures

	UNSATISFACTORY • LEVEL 1	BASIC • LEVEL 2
	The teacher displays dishonesty in interactions with colleagues, students, and the public. The teacher is not alert to students' needs and contributes to school practices that result in some students being ill served by the school. The teacher makes decisions and recommendations that are based on self-serving interests. The teacher does not comply with school and district regulations.	The teacher is honest in interactions with colleagues, students, and the public. The teacher's attempts to serve students are inconsistent, and unknowingly contribute to some students being ill served by the school. The teacher's decisions and recommendations are based on limited though genuinely professional considerations. The teacher must be reminded by supervisors about complying with school and district regulations.
CRITICAL ATTRIBUTES	• The teacher is dishonest. • The teacher does not notice the needs of students. • The teacher engages in practices that are self-serving. • The teacher willfully rejects district regulations.	• The teacher is honest. • The teacher notices the needs of students but is inconsistent in addressing them. • The teacher does not notice that some school practices result in poor conditions for students. • The teacher makes decisions professionally but on a limited basis. • The teacher complies with district regulations.
POSSIBLE EXAMPLES	• *The teacher makes some errors when marking the most recent common assessment but doesn't tell his colleagues.* • *The teacher does not realize that three of her neediest students arrive at school an hour early every morning because their mothers can't afford daycare.* • *The teacher fails to notice that one of his kindergartners is often ill, looks malnourished, and frequently has bruises on her arms and legs.* • *When one of her colleagues goes home suddenly because of illness, the teacher pretends to have a meeting so that she won't have to share in the coverage responsibilities.* • *The teacher does not file his students' writing samples in their district cumulative folders; it is time-consuming, and he wants to leave early for summer break.* • *And others...*	• *The teacher says, "I have always known my grade partner to be truthful. If she called in sick today, then I believe her."* • *The teacher considers staying late to help some of her students in after-school daycare but then realizes it would conflict with her health club class and so decides against it.* • *The teacher notices a student struggling in his class and sends a quick email to the counselor. When he doesn't get a response, he assumes the problem has been taken care of.* • *When the teacher's grade partner goes out on maternity leave, the teacher says "Hello" and "Welcome" to the substitute but does not offer any further assistance.* • *The teacher keeps his district-required gradebook up to date but enters exactly the minimum number of assignments specified by his department chair.* • *And others...*

PROFICIENT • LEVEL 3

The teacher displays high standards of honesty, integrity, and confidentiality in interactions with colleagues, students, and the public. The teacher is active in serving students, working to ensure that all students receive a fair opportunity to succeed. The teacher maintains an open mind in team or departmental decision making. The teacher complies fully with school and district regulations.

- The teacher is honest and known for having high standards of integrity.
- The teacher actively addresses student needs.
- The teacher actively works to provide opportunities for student success.
- The teacher willingly participates in team and departmental decision making.
- The teacher complies completely with district regulations.

- *The teacher is trusted by his grade partners; they share information with him, confident it will not be repeated inappropriately.*
- *Despite her lack of knowledge about dance, the teacher forms a dance club at her high school to meet the high interest level of her students who cannot afford lessons.*
- *The teacher notices some speech delays in a few of her young students; she calls in the speech therapist to do a few sessions in her classroom and provide feedback on further steps.*
- *The English department chair says, "I appreciate when ______ attends our after-school meetings; he always contributes something meaningful to the discussion."*
- *The teacher learns the district's new online curriculum mapping system and writes in all of her courses.*
- *And others...*

DISTINGUISHED • LEVEL 4

The teacher can be counted on to hold the highest standards of honesty, integrity, and confidentiality and takes a leadership role with colleagues. The teacher is highly proactive in serving students, seeking out resources when needed. The teacher makes a concerted effort to challenge negative attitudes or practices to ensure that all students, particularly those traditionally underserved, are honored in the school. The teacher takes a leadership role in team or departmental decision making and helps ensure that such decisions are based on the highest professional standards. The teacher complies fully with school and district regulations, taking a leadership role with colleagues.

- The teacher is considered a leader in terms of honesty, integrity, and confidentiality.
- The teacher is highly proactive in serving students.
- The teacher makes a concerted effort to ensure opportunities are available for all students to be successful.
- The teacher takes a leadership role in team and departmental decision making.
- The teacher takes a leadership role regarding district regulations.

- *When a young teacher has trouble understanding directions from the principal, she immediately goes to a more seasoned teacher—who, she knows, can be relied on for expert advice and complete discretion.*
- *After the school's intramural basketball program is discontinued, the teacher finds some former student athletes to come in and work with his students, who have come to love the after-school sessions.*
- *The teacher enlists the help of her principal when she realizes that a colleague has been making disparaging comments about some disadvantaged students.*
- *The math department looks forward to their weekly meetings; their leader, the teacher, is always seeking new instructional strategies and resources for them to discuss.*
- *When the district adopts a new Web-based grading program, the teacher learns it inside and out so that she will be able to assist her colleagues with its implementation.*
- *And others...*

THE
DANIELSON
GROUP

Made in the USA
Lexington, KY
19 October 2013